DISCARD

THE
HYGGE
LIFE

THE
HYGGE
LIFE

Embracing the nordic
art of coziness through
recipes, entertaining,
decorating, simple rituals,
and family traditions

GUNNAR KARL GÍSLASON
& JODY EDDY

TEN SPEED PRESS
California | New York

CONTENTS

Introduction 1

Starting the Day 9
Caring for Yourself 41
Staying In 51
Easy Gatherings and Holidays 75
Getting Out 131

Acknowledgments 156
Index 157

Recipes

STARTING THE DAY

Kleinur (Icelandic Beignets) 17

Spiced Buttermilk Fritters 20

Pancakes with Berries and Whipped Cream 24

Steel-Cut Oatmeal with Yogurt
and Spiced Roasted Apples 32

Rice Porridge 34

Rhubarb and Lemon Balm Smoothie 35

CARING FOR YOURSELF

Homemade Bath Salts 43

STAYING IN

Poached Eggs and Watercress with Pickled Shallots
and Horseradish 53

Fennel Salad with Blue Cheese and Walnuts 56

Smoked Cheese and Grilled Bread with Peppery Greens
and Lemon-Yogurt Dressing 58

Potato Soup with Smoked Haddock and Dill 60

Fried Fish with Almonds and Capers 62

Salmon with Baby Potatoes and Pine 64

Braised Pork Tenderloin with
Oyster Mushrooms and Parsnips 65

Bratwurst with Sauerkraut and Smashed Potatoes 66

Stove-Top Popcorn 69

Hot Chocolate 71

EASY GATHERINGS AND HOLIDAYS

Red Beet Salad with Hazelnuts, Pickled Onion, and Goat Cheese 82

Baked Cod with Celeriac Puree, Chorizo, and Caramelized Onions 85

Blackened Salmon with Cottage Cheese and Cider Vinaigrette 88

Lamb Stew 91

Braised Lamb Shanks with Bok Choy and Sweet-and-Sour Dill Oil 93

Grilled Rib Eyes with Herb Butter and Capers 95

Meringue Buttons 104

Kökur (Icelandic Cookies) 105

Ástarpungar (Love Balls) 107

Orange and Chocolate Cookies 108

Ginger Cookies 109

Laufabrauð 110

The Tom Cat 114

Birch Sour 116

Glögg 117

Berry Spritzers 118

House Bitters 119

GETTING OUT

Warm Potato Salad 136

Smørrebrød with Shredded Pork, Pickled Cabbage, and Horseradish Mayonnaise 137

Open-Faced Rye Bread Sandwiches with Cottage Cheese and Pickled and Salted Radishes 141

Marinated Herring on Rye Bread with Eggs and Shallot 142

Quick Rhubarb Pickles 148

INTRODUCTION

A Scandinavian winter is a long and frosty affair. It requires fierce resolve to brave the angry winds that gust inland from the ocean; to enjoy a few pale hours of sun before it slips beneath the horizon once more; to thrive in spite of adversity.

But it's more than a courageous heart and thick woolen socks that see Scandinavians joyfully through the dark, bleak season. Their spirits are enriched and hearts made buoyant by the concept of *hygge* ("hue-guh"). It's their winter elixir. It's the notion that taking care of yourself and those you love fortifies you with an invincible sense of well-being that no amount of snow or endless twilight can temper.

Loosely translated, the word *hygge* means "coziness," but for Scandinavians it means more than creating a warm and inviting space to live. It's about feeling cozy from the inside out and letting this sense of utter contentment permeate everything you encounter throughout the day, gloomy and gray as it may be. The word originated in Denmark, but the concept is fundamental to how all Scandinavian people live every day of the year. It's a concept that feels just right during the winter, but one they also carry into warmer months, when they spend long summer days hiking in forests and invite friends 'round for outdoor barbecues under a midnight sun.

Hygge is about creating a sanctuary of warmth and coziness that acts as a refuge for you and everyone you love. Inviting comforting elements into your day-to-day life is the essence of hygge. Grace, simplicity, and gratitude are the principles hygge practitioners adhere to for an abiding sense of well-being. The Scandinavian spirit overflows with hygge. Drinking hot spiced wine while wrapped in blankets by a glowing fire is hygge. A candlelit meal of warm comfort food with friends is hygge. A summer festival celebrating the longest day of the year with blazing campfires and live music is hygge. Wool socks, aromatic tea, and a good read at a cabin are hygge. A bakery with freshly baked bread is hygge. Bikes are more hygge than cars. Fluorescent lights are *never* hygge. Relaxing on the couch with a birch schnapps cocktail, your feet kept toasty nestled in the fur of a loving dog, is hygge.

Ultimately, hygge is meant to be felt. It's the art of creating intimacy and the comforting sense of togetherness in a candlelit room with a fire crackling and cheerful music playing in the background. It's eschewing an abundance of material possessions for wealth derived from friendship and solidarity. It's inviting friends for a picnic beside a river glistening in the summertime sun. It's taking care of your body through exercise that is not viewed as a burden but is enjoyed in the company of friends along a meandering woodland path. It's reveling in solitary moments spent reading a book while sipping a good cup of tea. Hygge means slowing down to capture a moment and to listen intently to the stories our loved ones have to share. In the springtime, hygge practitioners gather around outdoor tables flooded in sunshine to make merry over homemade sausages and a few rounds of beer.

The knowing hygge heart is light and gracious. It's filled with the wisdom of lifelong learning and the compounded gratification of tending others, from our tiniest babies to our oldest and frailest elders to our precious planet. It's also about caring for ourselves.

Hyggeligt is the adjectival form of hygge, and the word appears frequently in conversation in a region where, when the grip of winter is strongest, the sun never rises at all. Hygge finds its way into decorating, traveling, entertaining, and cooking. Homes in Scandinavia are decorated to look and feel hyggeligt with soft lighting, natural fibers, warm colors, and cozy blankets and pillows strewn all around.

It's hyggeligt to road trip with a group of friends instead of traveling alone. Staying in instead of going out is hyggeligt; if you do go out, you go to a place with a hyggeligt vibe where the lights are low, the food is comforting, and the conversations easy and relaxed. Hyggeligt dressing is about relaxed comfort, not sequins or scratchy fabrics.

There are events that inspire hyggeligt feelings, such as an orchestra playing classical music beneath a canopy of stars, the audience sitting on woolen rugs in hand-knitted socks, cups of hot cocoa in hand. Simple, slow-cooked meals, with flavors and ingredients that remind guests of their favorite childhood memories—that's the hygge way to cook. Creating atmosphere with retro tunes—that's the hygge way to entertain.

Hygge is about making time to pause and be grateful, taking a deep breath, turning off your gadgets, and listening to what nature has to tell you. It's about absorbing the laughter of your children and meaningfully listening to the stories our elders want to share with us. There is hygge wisdom to be gained there. It's about self-care and not feeling guilty about it. Loving ourselves is the first step to living the hygge life.

To truly embody the hygge lifestyle, you need to embrace its principles through each passing season in every aspect of your life. Certainly a relaxed cocktail party or cozy afternoon book club on a winter's day is prime hygge territory, but hygge can be applied to the office, too. The hygge workspace is organized and inviting, free from distractions but rich in inviting atmosphere. It's a place to accomplish meaningful work that gives you a sense of achievement and pride.

In Scandinavia, the government takes care of many of life's essential services, such as child care, education, and health care. The principles of hygge emerged throughout the region in part because its residents do not have to shoulder the burden of responsibility for many of life's expensive necessities—or bear the insecurity, uncertainty, and anxiety that accompany that burden. Feeling cared for has enabled Scandinavians to cultivate a tender approach to their relationships with others, with the planet, and with themselves. The good news is that the feeling of hygge is not exclusively reserved for Scandinavians, who have so brilliantly cultivated it over the centuries. Hygge is for everyone, because many of its basic tenets can easily and inexpensively be incorporated into daily life.

This book is about how to invite hygge into your own life, wherever you live in the world. It's a guide and inspiration for taking care of those you love and yourself. This book provides simple ways to discover and be your best hygge self.

The recipes are from Icelandic chef Gunnar Karl Gíslason, who has a knack for digging deep into his cozy hygge soul when he cooks. His food is simple and comforting, magically conjuring memories of childhood while at the same time inspiring optimism for the future.

Invigorating breakfasts that start the day right; addicting snacks to pair with craft beer and lively, thought-provoking discussions; simple soups with revitalizing flavors; comforting main dishes that don't require the cook to break a sweat; quirky cocktails that go down as smoothly as the conversation; and desserts that are as easy as they are fun—these are the benchmarks of Gunnar's hyggeligt cooking.

These dishes invite family and friends to gather 'round to savor simple flavors while enjoying a cozy day that warms up the psyche and makes everyone feel snuggled in and connected to people who love and support them.

STARTING THE DAY
BREAKFAST AND BRUNCH

A cozy morning enriches mind and body. Its fortifying rituals prepare us for whatever obstacles might arise in the ensuing hours. Morning is a time to map out what lies ahead, take time to care for yourself and others, wake up the imagination, and create a solid foundation for a successful day.

Developing a routine we can count on is one sure way to feel cozy the whole day through. It's the hygge way to do the morning. But there is more to a hygge morning than organization; it is also a time to arouse the creative mind and enliven the imagination. It's the luscious moment when everything seems possible, the day filled with promise. There is strength to be derived from a cozy morning routine. A brisk walk invigorates your body and charges your mind.

Treating those we love with tenderness the instant they open their sleepy eyes wraps our relationships in love and respect. And inviting friends and family into our homes at the beginning of the day to nourish them with healthful food and warm company is the hyggeligt way.

COFFEE AND TEA

There are so many ways to create a morning infused with the spirit of hygge. One of the best is to jumpstart the day with coffee or tea. It goes without saying that coffee and tea are the king and queen of most mornings throughout the world, and Scandinavia is no different. But even these fundamental sunrise mainstays can be made extraordinary with a little tweaking.

Our coffee of choice in Reykjavík is roasted and served at Reykjavík Roasters—a cozy café a few blocks from Gunnar's restaurant, Dill—where coffee creation is an art form. Reykjavík Roasters' owner is an award-winning barista from Iceland, who learned his craft at the Coffee Collective, a beloved Copenhagen coffee shop. He returned to Reykjavík with a passion for coffee that has turned his little café into the place to go for a perfect cuppa in a setting that is hygge through and through, with its basket of yarn and knitting needles on a shelf for anyone with a hankering, a vintage record player in one corner, and inviting nooks and crannies where coffee lovers settle in for a long morning of good conversation and cups of rich, perfectly brewed coffee.

With a bit of planning, the ritual of coffee or tea drinking can be elevated in your own home on even the busiest days, just as it is at Reykjavík Roasters. Stage everything you'll need the night before to avoid scrambling for the beans, filters, mugs, and spoons in the morning. Consider adding a sprinkle of ground cinnamon or nutmeg or swirling in a few drops of high-quality vanilla extract to elevate the usual routine. Buy a mug or traveling cup that feels unique, not utilitarian. Pick up coffee beans or tea during your travels to bring back memories from a relaxing vacation with each morning cup.

How to Make a Perfect Cup of Coffee or Tea at Home

COFFEE

Scandinavians love coffee. The average person enjoys around twenty pounds of coffee annually, with Finland in the lead at twenty-eight annual pounds per individual. Coffee breaks are an important part of the culture. In Finland and Sweden, a coffee break is called a *fika,* which is also the word for a coffee shop and even "coffee" itself. Norwegians and Danes refer to it as a *kaffeslabberas*; and for Icelanders, a coffee break is a *kaffiboð,* which, similar to a fika, is often accompanied by a light snack.

Selecting Coffee Beans

Be wary of inexpensive coffee beans. They are often of poor quality and dubious origin and will leave a bitter taste in your mouth. A good bean begins its life at the farm where it was cultivated. Look for "green," or unroasted, beans that can be traced back to their source and were grown sustainably by farmers who were paid a fair wage. Companies that source this kind of bean usually proudly display it on their label. Now, it's time for roasting; freshly roasted beans are ideal. Many coffee shops roast their beans in-house and are an excellent place to begin your search. The best bean flavor exists within the first two weeks of roasting, when the roasting oils are unspoiled and the overall flavor is broad and complex. Whole beans are essential because there is significant flavor loss once they are ground. Ground beans should be processed immediately. Invest in a coffee grinder or even an inexpensive spice grinder to grind beans yourself. Do not overgrind; your beans should be ground to order to avoid the bitterness that arises when the oils are overly agitated.

Brewing

There are many ways to brew a perfect cup of coffee. The result should be acidically well-balanced with a barely there, toasty-sweet note that emerges with each sip. It should have a slight velvety mouthfeel and a lingering sensation that is not bitter but is instead animated by subtle notes of nuttiness and depth. If you live in an area

where there is a high concentration of fluoride, calcium, or chlorine in your water, use neutral distilled water or filtered spring water instead. Here are a few options that result in multiple cups of flavorful coffee.

French Press

Equipment: French press, freshly ground coffee beans, very hot but not boiling water, and a spoon

- Depending on the size of your press, place approximately 6 tablespoons of freshly ground coffee beans into the press.

- Pour the hot water into the press; the ratio between liquid and grounds should be 10:1. Let this steep untouched for 5 minutes.

- Scrape the surface of the liquid with the spoon to remove accumulated froth and stray grounds.

- Using the plunger, gently press it down into the coffee to push the grounds to the bottom of the press. Pour into cups and serve.

Drip Filter

This is not the filtered coffee produced by a machine. Instead, it's the pour-over method that enables you to retain control of the speed at which the water is filtered through the grounds.

Equipment: paper filter (preferably unbleached), porcelain filter cone (available online and in most kitchen supply stores), receptacle such as a glass or ceramic decanter, hot but not boiling water, freshly ground coffee beans

- Arrange the filter inside the cone and place the cone over the receptacle. Pour hot water through the filter in order to rid it of its fibrous flavor note. Discard the water in the receptacle and rearrange the cone and filter on top.

- Place approximately 6 tablespoons of freshly ground coffee beans into the filter.

• Slowly pour 4 cups of hot water over the grounds. Pour only enough during this first stage to moisten (or bloom) your grounds. Give them about 30 seconds to adjust and then complete the process. The pour should last between 3 to 4 minutes. Enjoy!

TEA

Tea is the most widely consumed beverage in the world. It's encouraging to think that centuries of trial and error have gone into brewing a perfect cup. There are more than fifteen hundred varieties of tea on the planet, but only four categories of tea leaf. Herbal incarnations are technically not authentic "tea." More than six billion pounds of tea leaves are harvested annually around the world. The flavor notes of the highest-quality leaves can be compared to an esteemed bottle of wine. Look for tea that can be traced back to its source and is grown organically by farmers and pickers who are treated fairly. Tea leaf varieties include the following.

White: White tea is the rarest, most valuable, and most healthful of all tea varieties because it is the first stage in a tea leaf's growth, is relatively unprocessed, and is densely packed with nutrients such as antioxidants and amino acids. It is hand-harvested in the spring, contains the least amount of caffeine, and should have a silvery-white color. The best white teas taste slightly sweet, with a perfumed aroma.

Green: Green tea is the second stage in a tea leaf's life. It contains high levels of antioxidants and its flavor notes can vary depending upon how it is processed, which occurs after the white leaf loses its moisture content and takes on a limp appearance. In Japan, it is steamed, which gives it a pronounced herbal quality; in China, where it is traditionally roasted, its flavor profile is more pronounced. Both techniques are what give green tea leaves their distinctive, tightly rolled shape.

Oolong: Oolong tea, which falls between green and black tea, is produced in Asia, where the leaves are traditionally tossed in bamboo racks to mildly bruise them. This causes the tea's enzymes to react to oxygen and is what gives oolong its multifaceted flavor profile. Oolong that is darker in appearance will have a more caramelized flavor, whereas leaves that are lighter in color will have a more delicate floral note.

Black: Black tea is fully oxidized and is the most popular tea variety in the Western world. The iconic Earl Grey, Darjeeling, and English Breakfast are all black tea varieties. After the leaf is fully oxidized, it is fired to stop the process. The malty, robust flavor typically has notes of caramel and subtle dark chocolate.

Brewing Tea

The variety of tea leaf will determine the ratio of water to tea as well as its temperature and steeping time. If using a tea bag, the volume of tea is suitable for one cup of tea.

White tea: 2 teaspoons tea to 1 cup water at 160°F for 1 to 2 minutes

Green tea: 1 to 2 teaspoons tea to 1 cup water at 180°F for 3 to 5 minutes

Oolong tea: 1 to 2 teaspoons tea to 1 cup water at 175°F for 1 to 3 minutes

Black tea: 1 teaspoon tea to 1 cup water at 200°F for 3 to 5 minutes

Equipment, Process, and Tips

The equipment required to brew a quality cup of tea and the process itself are relatively simple. Here are a few tips to get you started.

Equipment: tea, infuser (if not using a tea bag), cup, and distilled water

Process: Place your tea bag or infuser in your cup and heat the water to the temperature outlined. Pour the water into your cup and steep as indicated. Remove the tea bag (or infuser) and enjoy.

Tips:

- Water that is too hot will flatten the tea's flavor.

- For stronger tea, do not increase the steeping time, as this can make the tea taste bitter. Instead, increase the volume of tea leaves.

Kleinur
(Icelandic beignets)

MAKES APPROXIMATELY 20 KLEINUR

4 cups all-purpose flour,
plus more for rolling

½ cup granulated sugar

1 tablespoon baking powder

1 teaspoon baking soda

1 teaspoon ground cardamom
(optional)

1 egg

½ cup buttermilk, or as needed

2 quarts peanut or canola oil

Confectioners' sugar for dusting

In Iceland, the *kleinur* ("kly-noor") pastry recipe has been passed down from one generation to the next for as long as anyone can remember. These addictive little treats, sweet and crunchy on the outside and airy and tender on the inside, are an integral part of chilly Icelandic mornings.

In a large bowl, sift together the flour, granulated sugar, baking powder, baking soda, and cardamom (if using). Add the egg and stir with a wooden spoon until incorporated. Add the buttermilk in increments until the batter comes together and resembles shaggy chocolate chip cookie dough; it should not be runny.

In a large, heavy-bottomed pot, heat the peanut oil to 350°F. Line a plate with a double layer of paper towels.

Lightly flour a clean work surface and rolling pin. Place the dough on the surface and gently roll out into a ½-inch-thick rectangle. (Add additional flour to the rolling pin if necessary.) Using a sharp paring knife, cut the kleinur into long diamond shapes. Lay a damp cloth towel over the kleinur so they do not dry out.

Working in batches so as not to crowd the surface of the oil, use a spatula to pick up each kleinur and carefully transfer to the oil. The batter will sink instantly, but rise to the surface within 2 to 3 minutes. Once it does, use a wooden spoon to turn gently and continue to fry until both sides are just golden brown, approximately 30 seconds more.

Using a slotted spoon, carefully transfer the kleinur to the prepared plate. Immediately sift confectioners' sugar over the kleinur. After the first batch, allow the oil to return to 350°F before repeating the process. Serve piping hot.

A MORNING HIKE

Coffee is one way to jumpstart the morning engine, but hiking or walking through your neighborhood is another way to fuel the day. If you'd like to combine the two, in Norway there's *turkaffe*, which translates as a coffee break while hiking. Movement through walking shakes off lethargy and perks up your brain. Morning exercise affords time to map out the hours ahead and find solutions to issues that might arise. Since the sun rises so early during the spring and summer months throughout Scandinavia, early morning hikes, commencing when the rest of the world is still sleeping, are not uncommon. We once hiked along the top of a glacier on the Snaefellsnes Peninsula in Iceland at 3:00 a.m., just as the July sun was beginning to rise. Scandinavians relish long springtime hikes after a winter of strolling in perpetual twilight. In Sweden, where it is said that the indigenous Sami people determine the length of their walk by the brews of coffee required to complete the trail, the 620-mile-long Skåneleden trail in the south of the country features well-posted signs, ancient forests, abundant wildlife, and quaint red cottages for lodging. In Norway, the breathtaking 12-mile-long Trolltunga walk features towering cliffs and culminates in "the tongue," a shard of rock perched high above the pristine water. Venturing to the edge of it is not for the faint of heart.

But you don't have to be in Scandinavia to relish a gratifying hike. Even a brisk morning walk through a non-rural area can inspire hygge moments. Instead of packing snacks, bring your wallet and see it as an opportunity to check out a new restaurant or coffee shop. Carry a lightweight collapsible bag in your pocket; you never know what discoveries you might make at a local market.

Spiced Buttermilk Fritters

MAKES APPROXIMATELY
20 FRITTERS

The crispy, golden brown exterior of these spiced fritters gives way to an airy interior with a subtle buttermilk tanginess. They call for cultured, not traditional thin, buttermilk; the cultured type provides the thick consistency needed to achieve a properly puffed fritter. They're the perfect recipe for a family breakfast because they are so versatile and have a way of pleasing everyone at the table. Later in the day, they are also nimble partners for bowls of hot soup, and they make lovely sandwiches when halved and stacked with sliced ham or turkey, pickles, your family's favorite cheese, and a spread of mustard and mayonnaise. For something sweet rather than savory, substitute cinnamon and nutmeg for the cumin and sprinkle them with confectioners' sugar as they emerge from the fryer—a Scandinavian version of a beignet. They are best served puffed and hot, but will hold up for a few hours when stored in a covered container at room temperature. On the weekend, serve with pints of cold beer for the adults and berry spritzers (see page 118) for the kids.

2 cups all-purpose flour,
plus more for rolling

1 tablespoon granulated sugar

1½ teaspoons baking soda

¼ teaspoon baking powder

½ teaspoon ground cumin

Kosher salt

1 tablespoon melted butter,
plus softened butter for serving
(optional)

1 cup cultured buttermilk

1 gallon canola oil

Slices of cheese, such as Swiss
or Harvarti, and prosciutto
for serving (optional)

In a large bowl, sift together the flour, sugar, baking soda, baking powder, cumin, and ½ teaspoon salt. Add the melted butter and buttermilk and stir with a wooden spoon until a shaggy dough forms. If the dough feels too tight, add a little water to loosen it in order to achieve a malleable but not runny consistency.

In a large, heavy-bottomed pot, heat the canola oil to 350°F. Line a few plates with a double layer of paper towels.

Dust a clean work surface with flour and roll out the dough ¾ inch thick. Cut the dough into squares approximately the size of a playing card. Using a slotted spoon, carefully drop the squares into the oil, one by one, being careful not to crowd the pot. The fritters will sink to the bottom but rise to the surface in about 3 minutes. Using the slotted spoon, gently flip them in the oil until they just begin to turn golden brown on all sides. Transfer to the prepared plates and sprinkle with salt. Repeat with the remaining fritter dough.

Serve piping hot alongside a bowl of softened butter and a plate of cheese and prosciutto.

Pancakes with Berries and Whipped Cream

Begin the morning with a large stack of hot Scandinavian pancakes glistening with melted butter, with bowls of fresh berries and freshly whipped cream on the side. It gets you as close to cozy as any breakfast can. Scandinavian pancakes are a distant cousin to bready American-style pancakes. In Nordic countries, they are nearly as thin as a sheet of paper, with a feathery-light texture similar to a crepe and a sweet finish. They're typically prepared using a specialty Scandinavian pancake pan, but a crepe pan or even a 9-inch nonstick sauté pan will work. Skilled Scandinavian pancake makers flip their pancakes by sending them airborne with a flick of the wrist. Mastering this step might require a few attempts, but don't be discouraged. Once you've acquired the pancake-flipping skill, it's a fun way to impress your friends and family. If you're not confident in your flipping abilities, use a large offset spatula.

MAKES APPROXIMATELY
20 PANCAKES (SERVES 4)

2 cups all-purpose flour

½ cup granulated sugar

1 teaspoon baking powder

½ teaspoon baking soda

2 eggs

2 tablespoons melted butter, plus softened butter for serving

¾ cup whole milk, or as needed

Canola oil for frying

Freshly whipped cream, blueberries or other fresh berries, and ground cinnamon for serving

In a large bowl, sift together the flour, sugar, baking powder, and baking soda. Add the eggs and melted butter and stir with a wooden spoon until incorporated. Add the milk, 1 tablespoon at a time, until the batter is smooth and thin.

Pour about ½ cup canola oil into a small bowl. Dip a paper towel into the oil and rub it over the surface of a Scandinavian pancake pan or crepe or nonstick sauté pan until the pan glistens. Set a plate next to the pan.

Warm the prepared pan over medium heat until it is hot but not smoking. Using a ladle, pour approximately ½ cup of batter onto the center of the hot pan to form a layer as thin as a playing card. Wearing an oven mitt, gently swirl the pan to evenly distribute the batter, then return it to the heat.

Watch the pancake carefully for tiny bubbles to form over the surface, about 3 minutes. When the bubbles start to form and approximately 1 inch of the edge looks drier than the interior and deepens in color, flip the pancake with a flick of your wrist, or use a large offset spatula.

After 2 minutes, use the spatula to lift one side of the pancake to see if the bottom is light golden brown. Once the pancake is ready, lift the pan and, using the spatula, slip the pancake onto the plate. Use a paper towel to carefully rub the hot pan with another slick of oil and return the pan to the stove, allowing about 30 seconds to heat back up. Repeat the process with the rest of the batter. Cover the finished pancakes with a cloth towel as you work to keep them as warm as possible. Once all the pancakes are cooked, distribute them on serving plates and serve alongside bowls of whipped cream and blueberries, with the cinnamon and softened butter.

BREAKFAST IN BED

The custom of breakfast in bed should not be relegated to Victorian times or *Downton Abbey* reruns. It's an unexpected surprise guaranteed to elicit feelings of joy and contentment in the recipient. It's a surefire way into their heart. Recipes should be handmade and easily portable; toast from homemade bread served with softened butter and favorite preserves, smoked salmon with poached eggs and blanched asparagus garnished with an edible flower, or homemade granola with a small pitcher of cold milk are all welcome meals to get the day started right. Round out the feast with spirit-lifting touches like fresh fruit, a tiny bowl of nuts, a small kettle of tea or pot of coffee, freshly squeezed juice, and a tiny jar of cinnamon-sugar. Looking to up the cozy ante? Add any (or all!) of the following to the tray, as space allows: the morning newspaper, a small votive candle with an uplifting aroma, an inspirational book of poetry, a handwritten quote, silverware tied with a ribbon, and a tiny vase of cheerful flowers.

Steel-Cut Oatmeal with Yogurt and Spiced Roasted Apples

SERVES 4

Breakfast is a sit-down affair in many Scandinavian households. It is often referred to as the *dagmál*, or "day-meal," and even on weekdays, it's a time-honored way for a family to fortify their bodies and spirits before venturing out into the world. Warm breakfasts like this one provide a comforting foundation to tackle the day ahead. Steel-cut oats are less refined than rolled oats, but both versions begin as oat groats. The difference is that steel-cut oats are cut into smaller pieces whereas rolled oats are flattened beneath a roller. Steel-cut oats take a bit longer to cook and are toothier and nuttier than their rolled counterparts. As well as being high in fiber and antioxidants, oats are credited with stabilizing blood-sugar levels and lowering cholesterol. Substitute pearl barley for the steel-cut oats for a Scandinavian twist; the cooking time will remain the same. Toasting the oats or barley before simmering will greatly enhance their flavor. Use Granny Smith apples in place of Red Delicious for a hint of tartness and, if desired, replace the hazelnuts with toasted pecans, walnuts, almonds, or pumpkin seeds. The original version of this recipe called for *skyr*, a thick Icelandic dairy product similar in texture to Greek yogurt. It's available in many grocery stores throughout the United States and is a nice Nordic alternative to the yogurt. It's also fat-free, which is an added healthful bonus. When Gunnar prepares this dish for his family, he sprinkles the finished oats with pine tree powder, which adds an earthy, slightly acidic flavor. It is not a requirement, but it certainly is a unique way to make this recipe Scandinavian, through and through.

Spiced Roasted Apples

2 Red Delicious apples, cored, halved, and each half quartered

1 tablespoon light brown sugar

¼ teaspoon ground cinnamon

¼ teaspoon ground cardamom

Pine Tree Powder

Needles from one 4-inch long-needled pine bough segment

Oatmeal

3 cups water

1 cup whole milk

1 tablespoon butter

1 cup steel-cut oats

1 teaspoon freshly grated lemon zest

Kosher salt

Yogurt for serving

Honey for serving

Coarsely chopped toasted hazelnuts for serving

To make the roasted apples: Preheat the oven to 400°F. Line a baking sheet with parchment paper.

In a large bowl, combine the apples, brown sugar, cinnamon, and cardamom and toss together until the apples are uniformly covered. Arrange the apples in a single layer on the prepared baking sheet. Bake until tender but still slightly firm, about 30 minutes. Turn the apples over halfway through the baking process. Remove from the oven and set aside.

To make the pine tree powder: Increase the oven temperature to 500°F. Line a baking sheet with parchment paper.

Rinse the pine needles under cold running water to remove excess sap and debris. Pat dry with paper towels. Arrange the pine needles on the prepared baking sheet. Bake until blackened, 10 to 12 minutes. When the needles are cool enough to handle, pulverize them in a spice grinder. Set aside. (The powder will keep in an airtight container for up to 2 weeks.)

To make the oatmeal: In a saucepan over medium heat, combine the water and milk and bring to a gentle simmer. (Do not bring it to a boil because milk scorches and boils over quickly.)

In a skillet over medium heat, melt the butter. Add the oats and toast, stirring constantly, until aromatic and golden brown, about 3 minutes.

Add the toasted oats and lemon zest to the simmering liquid and turn the heat to medium-low. Gently simmer, stirring occasionally, until all the liquid is absorbed and the oats are thick and creamy, about 30 minutes. Stir the oats more frequently during the last 10 minutes of cooking in order to prevent scorching. Remove from the heat and season with salt. Let rest for 5 minutes.

Gently stir the oatmeal, and spoon it into four bowls. Top with the roasted apples and yogurt, drizzle with honey, and sprinkle with hazelnuts and pine tree powder, if desired. Serve immediately.

Rice Porridge

A bowl of hot, sweet rice porridge on a brisk winter morning warms you up from the inside out. This no-fuss version is baked at a low temperature, meaning once it's in the oven you can get on with your daily routine without fretting over it. It's a lovely brunch dish, since it's both comforting and easy to prepare ahead of time. As it bakes, a thin skin will form on the surface; this should be stirred back in two or three times during the cooking process. In Iceland, fried slices of *slátur* ("slae-toor"), or blood pudding, are typically served on the side, but for a more hyggeligt way to fancy-up this porridge, we offer a variety of garnish and seasoning ideas. For the adult version, a splash of brandy or cognac is sure to set the morning heart a-flutter.

SERVES 4

1¼ cups short-grain rice

5½ cups whole milk, plus more for serving

1 tablespoon granulated sugar

⅔ cup butter, cut into ½-inch cubes, plus more for serving

½ cup raisins (optional)

¼ cup pumpkin seeds (optional)

½ cup berries, such as blueberries or raspberries (optional)

¼ cup nuts, such as walnuts or hazelnuts (optional)

Pinch of ground star anise, cinnamon, nutmeg, or cloves (optional)

Kosher salt

Cinnamon-sugar for sprinkling (optional)

Preheat the oven to 325°F.

In a large, heavy-bottomed pot with a lid, combine the rice, milk, granulated sugar, and butter cubes and stir to mix. Bake, partially covered, for 1 hour, then stir in the raisins, pumpkin seeds, berries, nuts, and/or star anise (if using). A skin will form on the surface approximately 45 minutes into baking; stir it into the porridge using a wooden spoon and repeat the process once or twice more before removing from the oven. Season with salt.

Spoon the porridge into bowls, top with a slice of butter, drizzle with milk, and sprinkle with cinnamon-sugar, if desired, before serving.

Rhubarb and Lemon Balm Smoothie

Scandinavians love to begin their mornings with a healthful smoothie. This one incorporates rhubarb and lemon balm, two ingredients found in the countryside throughout the region. Lemon balm, which is often referred to in Scandinavia as Melissa, contains properties that are natural relaxants. Because of this, it has been appreciated for centuries as a stress remedy and is also used as a mosquito repellent in the spring and summer. This native European herb has a mild, lemony flavor, with leaves similar in shape and size to mint. In this recipe, frozen rhubarb is used because it is easier to blend, but feel free to substitute fresh rhubarb if it is available. The almond milk could be switched out for coconut, soy, cashew, or regular milk and the honey could be swapped out for agave or maple syrup. For an extra dose of nutrition, add a teaspoon of flax seeds, chia seeds, or raw cacao before blending. For a little extra zing, add a teaspoon of finely chopped fresh ginger.

SERVES 2

2 cups frozen chopped rhubarb

12 lemon balm leaves, coarsely chopped, plus whole leaves for garnish (optional)

2 cups plain Greek yogurt

3 tablespoons honey

1 cup almond milk, plus more as needed

Combine the rhubarb, lemon balm, yogurt, honey, and almond milk in a blender and puree at high speed until smooth. Add additional milk to achieve the desired consistency. Pour into two glasses; garnish with lemon balm leaves, if desired. Serve immediately.

A Hygge Brunch

Once, during a summer trip to the east of Iceland where Gunnar's family maintains a holiday home, he got us involved in brunch preparation by handing over a pair of scissors and a basket lined with a linen napkin and giving instructions to snip angelica from the bush growing near the property. It was so rewarding to gather 'round the table and sprinkle our freshly harvested angelica over chopped boiled potatoes dripping with melted butter and seasoned with crunchy sea salt. The hygge takeaway from that morning is that guests are happy to complete a brunch task—especially when it contributes to eating something irresistible.

Hosting a brunch shouldn't be stressful for the guests or the cook. Prepare as much as possible the night before, and leave the fancy omelet recipes for another time.

The evening before your brunch

- Prepare a music playlist.

- Purchase and place flowers in vases.

- Clean, polish, and arrange your serviceware, including required cooking equipment.

- If serving cocktails, prepare the mixer and arrange anything else you will need—such as a shaker, spirits, glasses, bitters, and garnishes—on the counter so they're ready to go.

- If serving tea, set up the tea station with a variety of options.

- If you are using cloth napkins, roll and secure them with a decorative ribbon, if desired.

- If you will be serving a cheese and charcuterie plate, slice and arrange items on a serving platter, cover securely with plastic wrap, and refrigerate.

- Fill small, decorative bowls with items such as jam, honey, pickles, and olives; cover securely with plastic wrap; and refrigerate.

- Pick up pastry and bread from the bakery, if you're not baking it yourself.

On the day of your brunch

- Light scented candles with an invigorating aroma.

- Instead of frying greasy items like sausages and bacon, bake them for a cleaner and healthier option.

- Set the table, prepare the cocktail station and buffet area (if a buffet will be offered).

- Set the butter out so it comes to room temperature before guests arrive.

- Grind coffee beans and prepare the required equipment.

- Light a fire if you have a fireplace, turn on the music, and wait for your guests to arrive.

BRUNCH THEME IDEAS

- A classic Southern brunch: shrimp and grits, hush puppies, roasted corn soup, crab cakes with spicy remoulade, fluffy biscuits, and Southern cocktails like mint juleps or old-fashioneds

- A farm brunch: pancakes with farm-fresh berries or stone fruit served with clotted cream; farm-egg frittata with smoked bacon and fresh herbs; yogurt parfait with a topping station that includes seeds, nuts, fresh fruit, honey, and granola; mimosas with freshly squeezed juice

- A tea party: chilled soup such as gazpacho or cucumber buttermilk, crackers and a soft cheese such as brie along with prosciutto, peaches and syrupy balsamic vinegar, a variety of open-faced sandwiches (see page 140), a variety of tea options with aromatic sugars (see page 81), lavender lemonade (spiked or unspiked) and berry spritzers (see page 118)

CARING FOR YOURSELF

You can best nurture others when you have carved out the time to care for yourself. Winter can be isolating in Scandinavian nations, where the sun never rises, hovering on the horizon in an afternoon twilight before slipping away again. We can find comfort in solidarity with others during those frigid winter months, but there is also gratification in being alone. Taking time for self-care is the first step toward loving others—and everyone we encounter will sense this affirmation of love.

Icelanders view a weekly trip to one of the many geothermal pools to cleanse the body of toxins as a pleasure rather than a chore. They also relish a long walk to the seacoast or a brisk swim in the ocean.

Spa visits throughout many parts of Scandinavia are a routine aspect of taking care of the body and spirit. Seaweed wraps, massage, and silica mud masks for the body and face are common treatments, and it can't be denied that many Scandinavians glow from the inside out. Spa treatments at home are easy and relatively inexpensive to introduce into your weekly routine. A hygge spa experience at home includes scented candles with an aroma evoking the outdoors, such as moss or pine. Soaking in a bath of Epsom salt perfumed with invigorating essential oils is an easy way to introduce a desirable pause into your life. If you double the batch, it also makes a welcome gift for a loved one who could also use a little tender care.

Grooming is another aspect of Scandinavian culture that should not be overlooked. Old-school barbers complete with vintage barbershop tools are where some Scandinavian men look for a proper shave. It's not only about lathering up the face for a routine beard trim, it's also about sharing a chat with a barber who has sometimes been a feature of a family for multiple generations. Contemporary beard oils with notes of birch or tobacco are prevalent in the young Scandinavian man's grooming repertoire. Gunnar's preferred barber in Reykjavík has set up shop in the back of a haberdashery, which means Gunnar not only maintains a neatly trimmed, properly nourished beard, he sometimes has a new tweed vest tucked under his arm when he leaves the store.

Cozy spaces are also essential to caring for yourself. A home office or reading corner is easily and inexpensively transformed from a humdrum, utilitarian space into an inviting hygge realm that will not only spark new ideas but also entice you to linger. Taking care of yourself through the preparation of healthful recipes, taking time to invigorate your body, and setting aside a few minutes each day to take a breath and feel grateful in an environment evoking comfort and peace are the first steps you should take to achieving your best hygge life.

Homemade Bath Salts

Homemade bath salts are easy to make, soothe inflamed skin, and relieve stress instantly. Epsom salt contains magnesium, which helps relieve aching muscles and swollen joints. A few drops of essential oil provide an aromatherapy benefit; for example, try peppermint oil for invigoration, sandalwood oil for relaxation, and eucalyptus oil for stress relief. Add one cup of your homemade salt to a hot bath while the water is running, and swish your hand through the water for a few moments to dissolve the salt before you climb into the tub.

MAKES 6 CUPS

2 cups Epsom salt

4 cups coarse sea salt

24 drops essential oil of your choice

In a large bowl, combine the Epsom salt and sea salt and stir with a wooden spoon until incorporated. Add the essential oil and stir once more until the salt is infused with its aroma. Keep the salt in a dry glass jar with a secure lid.

A TRIP TO THE SAUNA

Scandinavians have mastered the art of the sauna, and so can you. There's no better way to counter a blustery, dreary winter day than to take a trip to the sauna. And it's even more fun with a friend. Bring along a towel scented with eucalyptus oil to perk yourself up in between sessions and, for hydration, a bottle of water infused with a few lemon wedges and a mint sprig. Heat the stones over the highest-possible temperature, keeping them dry for the first round. Have cozy robes, slippers, and towels ready to sink into after the session. Get naked or wear a towel, depending upon how close your friendship is, and savor the dry heat as it opens up your pores. Take deep breaths, close your eyes, and relax. Every ten minutes or so, step outside if it's a chilly day or take a cold shower before beginning another session.

In the woodland home saunas of Scandinavia, pine or birch boughs are often gathered and arranged on the hot stones for a lovely aromatherapy session. If you have access to a home sauna and birch or maple twigs affixed with plenty of leaves are available, it's fun to have a friend with you so you can gently beat each other with them to truly bring out your inner Scandinavian. It's sure to make you laugh, but it's also a rustic massage that will get your circulation flowing and flush toxins from your skin. Conclude your sauna with a cold shower, but don't don your robe until you've stopped sweating. Those beads of liquid are filled with toxins. Let them flow away.

A COZY NOOK

In our chaotic world of hurry and noise, where we are perpetually connected to countless people, alerted by bells and beeps, we sometimes forget the solace of solitude. Even the most social of us crave a break from the sensory overload every once in a while. Take time for a quiet afternoon on your own every now and again. A crackling fire or a few candles will illuminate the space and clear your mind of the built-up clutter. Don't plan to do anything but simply be, preferably with a hot cup of tea or coffee in your hand, a blanket wrapped around your shoulders, and, in the ideal hygge world, snow or rain falling gently outside the window. Ponder all the wondrous things you're grateful for in that calm and enveloping moment of solitude.

The physical book is sometimes relegated to second fiddle in our contemporary world of gadgets and electronic screens. But there is no better way to reconnect with your imagination and rejuvenate creativity and lose yourself than reading in a cozy nook. Line a comfortable chair—preferably next to a natural light source and a blooming houseplant or fresh flowers—with sheepskin or an enveloping blanket, position a footstool in front of it, pull on your softest slippers, brew a cup of tea, light a candle, and open up your favorite book and surrender to the swish of its turning pages.

GROOMING THE HYGGE WAY

Men may wish to seek out a traditional barber who knows how to administer a proper shave that will leave you feeling polished and reborn. For those with a mustache and/or beard, a refined trim frames one's face, and scented beard oils perk up the senses and condition the skin. In Reykjavík, there are several old-school barbers who dress for work in a tweed vest and offer their clients a perfect shave while engaging them in a conversation, often continuing a discussion that has been going on for years. These traditional establishments are part barber shop, part haberdashery; along with your haircut, you can get your new pants hemmed and find a replacement trim for your wool hat. Gunnar's barber not only trims his beard but concludes his work by singing a classic tune familiar to every Icelander since childhood, accompanying himself on his guitar.

STAYING IN
WEEKNIGHT MEALS AND ACTIVITIES
FOR COZY NIGHTS AT HOME

Home meals on weekends can be long affairs that may include slow braises that fill the house with a tempting aroma. Quicker weeknight dishes also have a place when your family is tucking in for the evening. Recipes do not have to be complex when you stay in since it's as much about inspiring solidarity by hanging out with one another as it is about the menu.

Comfort food is the way to go when you're staying in on a weeknight. These recipes are easy to prepare and, because comfort food is usually a crowd-favorite that never loses its magic, talking about what will be on the dinner table that night is a compelling incentive to rush home after school.

Preparing the weeknight meal together triggers laughter and an easy sense of belonging. For children, cooking is also a way to build a life skill that is sorely lacking in our rushed society. Put someone in charge of vegetable prep, another in charge of preparing the proteins and seeing the cooking through from beginning to end, and assign someone else to measure out the *mise en place*, the ingredients required to prepare the meal. Whoever finishes up their task first is in charge of setting the table. Rotate who is responsible for cleanup so it doesn't become a dreaded chore. If your kids take their lunches to school, pack up the leftovers and tuck them into the lunch bags. If you've enjoyed something substantial like a roasted chicken or braised pork, transform it into sandwiches that are sure to elicit envy at the school lunch table.

Movie night (see page 68) is an ideal staying-in activity. Think through the evening ahead of time by planning a theme, inviting over neighbors and friends, and offering a fun but easy to pull together snack table—essential keys to a successful gathering. No film extravaganza would be complete without popcorn, including the addictive toppings.

Staying home sometimes means inviting a loved one over for date night. It could also mean carving out time with your partner or spouse to rekindle your spark by scheduling a well-planned romantic evening. There are so many ways to spend time at home together. Children grow up and move on to new life stages, couples require salvation from a humdrum routine, and we all need a relaxing night at home filled with laughter, camraderie, and love. The time is now.

Poached Eggs and Watercress with Pickled Shallots and Horseradish

There's a reason horseradish makes your nose tingle and your eyes water. It's a member of the wasabi and mustard family, and when it's sliced or grated, like in this recipe, the disturbed plant cells unleash a chemical that releases mustard oil, a component that is irritating to the eyes and sinuses. But much like wasabi, the electrifying sensation disappears in an instant, leaving behind a bright, mustardy note. Horseradish was introduced to Scandinavia during the Renaissance era, and it has become a mainstay in recipes that range from seafood to beef to fresh green dishes like this one. It has been used for thousands of years in western Asia and southern Europe, where it originated, to lower blood pressure, fortify the bones and heart, encourage weight loss, and treat respiratory ailments. The slightly sweet pickled shallots in this dish play well with the bite of the horseradish and peppery watercress, while the poached egg with its runny yolk mellow out the strong, bold personalities of the other ingredients. For additional texture and flavor, garnish each bowl with a handful of crumbled smoked bacon before placing the egg on top.

SERVES 4

Pickled Shallots

2 medium shallots, peeled and thinly sliced into rings

1 cup warm water

1 tablespoon apple cider or distilled white vinegar

1 tablespoon granulated sugar

1 pinch kosher salt

To make the pickled shallots: Place the shallots in a small nonreactive bowl. In a second bowl, combine the water, vinegar, sugar, and salt and whisk until the sugar and salt dissolve. Pour the liquid over the shallots and let stand at room temperature for 30 minutes. Drain the shallots before serving, reserving 2 tablespoons of pickling liquid for assembly.

Line a plate with paper towels.

continued

Poached Eggs and Watercress with Pickled Shallots and Horseradish

2 tablespoons apple cider or distilled white vinegar

4 eggs

Kosher salt

1 tablespoon grapeseed oil

4 cups loosely packed watercress

¼ cup toasted sunflower seeds

Fresh horseradish for serving

Add water into a saucepan until it reaches 4 inches up the sides. Add the vinegar and bring to a boil, then lower the heat to a lazy simmer. Crack each egg into a separate ramekin. Gently tip one of the eggs into the simmering water, then repeat with a second egg, trying not to let the eggs touch. The egg whites will begin to coagulate almost immediately. After about 3 minutes, use a slotted spoon to carefully transfer each egg to the prepared plate. Season with salt. Bring the liquid back up to boiling, then return to a gentle simmer and repeat with the remaining eggs.

In a small bowl, whisk together the reserved pickling liquid and grapeseed oil to make a vinaigrette.

In a large bowl, toss together the watercress and vinaigrette and season with salt. Divide evenly among four serving bowls. Top with the pickled onions and sprinkle with sunflower seeds. Carefully place an egg on top of each bowl and, using a Microplane, grate fresh horseradish over everything. Serve immediately.

Fennel Salad with Blue Cheese and Walnuts

SERVES 4

1 fennel bulb,
cored and thinly sliced

1 tablespoon
apple cider vinegar

1 tablespoon canola oil

Kosher salt

½ cup coarsely
chopped walnuts

1 tablespoon butter

2 slices day-old sourdough
bread, crusts removed and
bread torn into bite-size pieces

2 cups salad greens
of choice, such as mesclun,
arugula, or baby spinach

One 4-ounce wedge of
blue cheese, crumbled

Finely sliced radishes
for garnish

Edible flower blossoms
for garnish (optional)

This is the perfect salad for a casual lunch with friends because it comes together in a few minutes and most of the elements can be prepared up to a day before. It's also ideal for winter since all of the ingredients are available year-round. Substitute goat cheese for a less-funky finish or a buttery cheese like manchego to complement the acidity of the vinegar.

Preheat the oven to 325°F and line two baking sheets with aluminum foil.

In a small bowl, toss together the fennel, apple cider vinegar, and canola oil until the fennel is glistening. Season with salt. Arrange on one of the prepared baking sheets.

Bake the fennel until it is tender, about 12 minutes. Let cool to room temperature.

Meanwhile, arrange the walnuts on the second baking sheet and bake until toasted, about 6 minutes. Watch carefully, as they can brown quickly.

In a nonstick skillet over medium heat, melt the butter. Add the bread pieces and fry until they are slightly crispy and golden brown, about 4 minutes. Season with salt.

Evenly distribute the greens among four plates. Top with the fennel, walnuts, and toasted bread and then garnish with the blue cheese, radishes, and flower blossoms, if desired, before serving.

Smoked Cheese and Grilled Bread with Peppery Greens and Lemon-Yogurt Dressing

SERVES 4

Salads are the ultimate self-care recipe, affording a blank canvas to populate with healthful ingredients that quell our hunger pangs without weighing us down. This salad is loaded with assertive flavors that perk up the palate, showcasing a smoky note enhanced by a vibrant tanginess that eventually gives way to a peppery finish. For a rustic flourish, tear the bread into generous chunks before grilling it. This dish calls for walnuts but feel free to substitute whichever nut or seed you prefer. Walnuts have a long history in Scandinavia; even though hazelnuts are the only indigenous nut in the region, walnuts have been imported from other parts of Europe since the Viking era. To prepare the cheese shavings, use a vegetable peeler to create large curly ribbons. Smoked Gouda is an easily sourced cheese in most grocery stores; but for a twist, look for a soft Danish cheese called *rygeost* in Scandinavian specialty stores. This is a cow's milk and buttermilk cheese with a texture that is similar to ricotta. It's aged for twenty-four hours and the last steps in its preparation are to quickly smoke it over hay and nettles and then to sprinkle it with caraway seeds. It's difficult to find, so be sure to snatch it up if you ever run across it. For a heartier salad, add softly poached eggs for a gloriously sunny finish.

Lemon-Yogurt Dressing

¾ cup plain Greek yogurt

1 tablespoon honey

1 tablespoon freshly squeezed
lemon juice

1 tablespoon butter

1½ cups hand-torn
sourdough bread chunks

Kosher salt

4 cups loosely packed arugula

½ cup coarsely chopped
toasted walnuts

½ cup smoked Gouda shavings

4 poached eggs
(see page 53; optional)

To make the dressing: In a small bowl, whisk together the yogurt, honey, and lemon juice until smooth and creamy.

Line a plate with paper towels.

In a skillet over medium heat, melt the butter. Add the bread chunks and then sauté until toasty and golden brown along the edges of the nooks and crannies. Transfer to the prepared plate to soak up any excess butter. Season with salt.

In a large decorative bowl, toss together the dressing, bread, and arugula until the dressing clings in a velvety white film to each of the leaves. Sprinkle with the walnuts and smoked Gouda and top with the eggs, if desired. Serve family style.

Potato Soup with Smoked Haddock and Dill

SERVES 4

Cooking for yourself doesn't have to be a depressing undertaking. A hygge meal for one is not an afterthought. It can be conjured up through candlelight, a colorful vase containing a sprig of leaves, a glass of crisp white wine, and a magazine you've been meaning to catch up on. Everyone loves soup, and for good reason. There is joy in a pot of soup bubbling away on the stove top, and I can think of no better way to counter a snowy day than with a hand-warming bowlful of comfort. When you know you'll be coming home to hot soup at day's end, it's a pleasure to be out and about in the winter chill. This creamy potato soup is elevated with the addition of smoked haddock and the brightness of dill. Haddock is popular throughout Scandinavia, but if you don't have easy access to it, any smoked fish, such as cod or salmon, will do. The soup reheats well, but be sure to add the smoked fish only when you're ready to serve, or the smokiness will overpower the soup's delicate flavor. For a variation, swap out the potatoes for parsnips or carrots, or a combination of all three. The soup will keep in a covered container in the refrigerator for up to 3 days or frozen indefinitely.

4 tablespoons butter

2 medium leeks, white and pale green parts only, rinsed thoroughly and thinly sliced

1 small onion, coarsely chopped

2 large russet potatoes, peeled and coarsely chopped

3 cups chicken stock

⅔ cup heavy cream

1 cup whole milk

½ cup sour cream, plus more for garnish (optional)

5 ounces boneless smoked haddock, cod, or salmon, cut into bite-size pieces

Sea salt

Finely chopped fresh dill for garnish (optional)

In a large soup pot over high heat, melt 2 tablespoons of the butter. Add the leeks and onion and sauté until transparent, about 6 minutes. Add the potatoes and sauté for 3 minutes more. Then, add the chicken stock and bring to a vigorous simmer. Turn the heat to medium-low, add the heavy cream and milk, and simmer gently until the potatoes are tender, about 50 minutes. Either transfer the soup to a countertop blender or use an immersion blender to carefully puree until smooth. Be careful to prevent the hot soup from splattering; work in batches if necessary. If using a countertop blender, remove the lid's center plug so steam can escape, but drape a dish towel over it to contain any splashes. When done, return the soup to the pot.

Add the remaining 2 tablespoons butter, the sour cream, and smoked fish to the pot; return to high heat until the soup comes to a simmer, then lower the heat and simmer gently until the fish is warmed through. Season with salt, ladle the soup into bowls, and garnish with dill and sour cream, if desired, before serving.

Fried Fish with Almonds and Capers

SERVES 4

Eight 6-ounce skinned
and deboned fish fillets
(flounder, sole, or cod),
cut into 2-inch pieces

Sea salt

All-purpose flour for dredging

¾ cup butter,
cut into ½-inch cubes

1 tablespoon freshly
grated lemon zest

2 tablespoons capers

¼ cup slivered almonds

2 tablespoons
finely chopped chives

Finely chopped herbs such as
parsley, tarragon, or lemon
verbena for garnish (optional)

Lemon wedges and
sour cream for serving

This is a quick meal to pull together on a busy family weekend at home, a lighter incarnation of fried fish that should appeal to all ages. Chives harvested from the family garden are the perfect garnish that will excite the kids who grew them. A white fish that holds together, such as flounder, sole, or cod, works well—and don't skip the brown butter. It deepens the flavor, its caramelized notes a sweet counterpoint to the lemon zest acidity and the mouth-puckering capers. Toasted sunflower seeds or hazelnuts are good substitutes for the almonds.

Line a plate with a double layer of paper towels.

Season the fish with salt and dredge in flour, shaking off the excess. Set aside.

In a sauté pan over high heat, melt about 2 tablespoons of the butter. Add the fish, a few pieces at a time, and fry; do not crowd the pan. When the fish is golden brown on one side, about 3 minutes, flip over, ideally using a fish spatula, and continue to fry until cooked through and golden brown, about 3 minutes more. Transfer to the prepared plate and sprinkle with salt. Scrape up and discard any bits remaining in the pan. Add 1 tablespoon butter to the pan if necessary and continue to fry the rest of the fish. Once the last batch is finished, scrape up and discard the remaining brown bits.

Add the remaining butter, the lemon zest, capers, and almonds to the pan and sauté until the butter sauce is golden brown.

Arrange the fish on a large communal platter, drizzle with the brown butter sauce, garnish with the chives and herbs, if desired, and serve with lemon wedges and a bowl of sour cream alongside.

Salmon with Baby Potatoes and Pine

A fish fillet is a lovely solo meal because it's so easy to prepare, and it's a splendid way to conclude a spa day because it's a healthful choice that won't weigh you down. This recipe originally called for arctic char, an easy fish to source in Iceland, but it can be challenging to find in other places. Salmon is an ideal substitute, but any fish with sturdy flesh, such as halibut or cod, will do. The fish is slathered in smoked butter before being bundled up with the pine and then baked. If you can find smoked butter, by all means grab it; if not, regular butter works too.

An 8-inch-long pine sprig makes this dish feel festive. It is easy to prepare; simply wash under cold running water for a few minutes to remove any debris and sap, then pat dry with a cloth towel.

SERVES 1

1 cup small new potatoes

One 8-ounce skin-on salmon fillet, deboned

Sea salt

2 tablespoons smoked butter

1 tablespoon salted butter

Bring a small pot of salted water to a boil. Add the potatoes, lower the heat to a gentle simmer, and cook uncovered until the potatoes are fork tender, about 12 minutes.

Preheat the oven to 450°F.

Place the salmon fillet lengthwise on a sheet of aluminum foil three times as long as the fillet. Sprinkle with salt and top with the smoked butter and a pine sprig. Wrap the salmon in the foil to form a loose yet tightly secured packet and bake for 12 minutes.

Meanwhile, drain the potatoes, transfer to a plate, top with the salted butter, and season with salt.

Once the salmon is cooked, set the packet aside for 4 minutes before carefully opening, to prevent the steam from burning your skin. Discard the pine sprig and serve the salmon alongside the potatoes.

Braised Pork Tenderloin with Oyster Mushrooms and Parsnips

This is a refined dish that looks impressive without too much fuss. It's a comforting meal that invites tucking into over a long conversation illuminated by glimmering candlelight, with plenty of wine.

SERVES 6

3 pounds pork tenderloin, trimmed

Kosher salt

5 tablespoons butter

1 small white onion, halved and thinly sliced

6 garlic cloves, thinly sliced

2 cups dry red wine

2 cups chicken stock, plus more as needed

3 parsnips, peeled and coarsely chopped

2 thyme sprigs

Apple cider vinegar for seasoning

1 bunch oyster mushrooms

½ cup pickled onion (see page 82)

Season the tenderloin with salt.

In a nonstick skillet over high heat, melt 2 tablespoons of the butter. Add the tenderloin and brown on all sides. Remove from the heat and let rest.

In a heavy-bottomed pot over medium heat, melt 1 tablespoon butter. Add the white onion and garlic and sauté until the onion is translucent. Then add the wine and simmer until reduced by half. Add the chicken stock and the tenderloin. Partially cover, turn the heat to medium-low, and let simmer until the loin is cooked through, about 90 minutes. Transfer the tenderloin to a plate and let rest, flipping once during this period to evenly distribute the juices. Return the pot to medium heat and reduce the cooking juices by half. If you like a smoother sauce, strain through a fine-mesh sieve.

Wipe out the skillet, return to medium-high heat, and melt another 1 tablespoon butter. Add the parsnips and sauté until golden brown and tender, about 20 minutes. Add a little chicken stock if necessary to prevent scorching. Add the thyme and then season with vinegar and salt. Remove the parsnips from the pan with a slotted spoon and keep warm.

Add the remaining 1 tablespoon butter and the mushrooms to the skillet, and sauté until golden brown and nearly crispy, about 9 minutes.

Slice the tenderloin into 1-inch pieces. Spoon the parsnips and mushrooms onto each dinner plate. Top with a few slices of tenderloin, garnish with the pickled onion, and drizzle with the reduced cooking juices before serving.

Bratwurst with Sauerkraut and Smashed Potatoes

SERVES 4

8 red bliss potatoes, skin on

5 tablespoons butter

1 tablespoon Dijon mustard (use stone-ground if you prefer something less tangy), plus more for serving

Apple cider vinegar for seasoning

Sea salt

4 large bratwurst or other hearty sausage

2 cups prepared sauerkraut

This is a perfect winter-holiday lunch meal that requires little fuss and delivers a hearty result. The original recipe calls for homemade sausage along with sauerkraut that takes six months to prepare. An easy alternative is store-bought kraut and the finest sausages you can find. Serve with high-quality mustard, and substitute parsnips for the potatoes if your family prefers something sweeter. When preparing the potatoes, don't use a potato masher or the results will be too smooth.

Bring a pot of salted water to a vigorous simmer over high heat. Turn the heat to medium, add the potatoes, and cook until just tender, 14 to 16 minutes. Drain the potatoes and transfer to a medium bowl. When the potatoes are cool enough to handle, add 2 tablespoons of the butter and the mustard and smash with a fork, preserving a chunky texture. Season with vinegar and salt.

Line a plate with paper towels.

While the potatoes are cooking, in a nonstick skillet over medium-high heat, melt 2 tablespoons butter. Add the bratwurst and fry until cooked through and golden brown. Drain on the prepared plate. Add the sauerkraut to the skillet along with the remaining 1 tablespoon butter and sauté until warmed through.

Place a bratwurst on each dinner plate and spoon some of the kraut and the potatoes alongside. Serve with additional mustard.

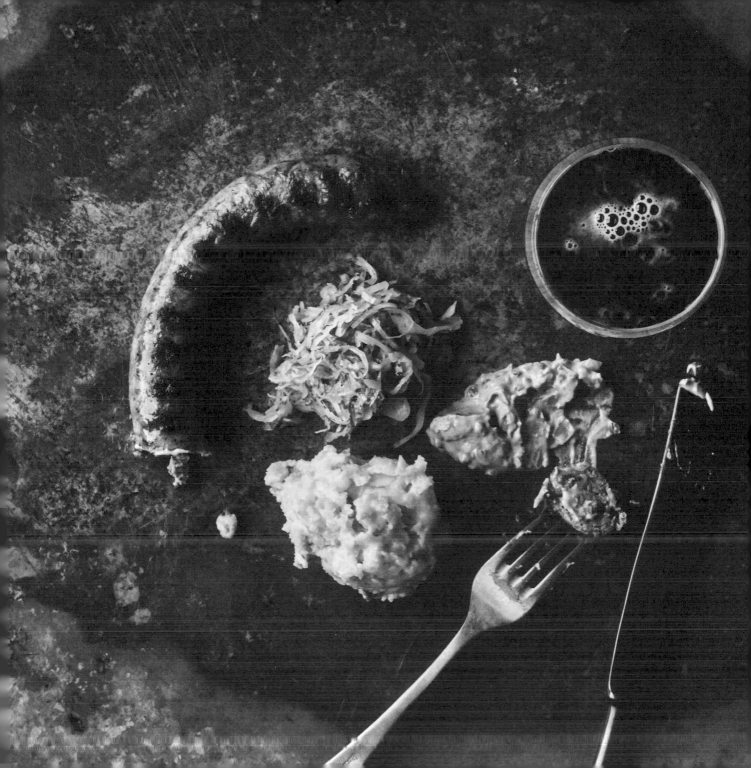

MOVIE NIGHT

Movie night is a fun evening for every generation. If you're hosting a large group, print admission tickets to be delivered ahead of time and have one of your kids collect them at the door. Pile pillows, cushions, and blankets on the floor to encourage relaxation. Between movies, play a game of film trivia or charades related to the theme and offer boxes of classic movie candy as prizes.

Consider hosting a themed movie night in order to keep the evening focused and build snacks, dinner, drinks, and bingo and trivia games around it.

Ideas include

- Romantic comedies that make you cry

- Movies with main characters who started out with nothing and ended up with the world

- Movies with animals as the primary characters

- Movies where the protagonist saves the planet

- A Bollywood-themed movie night that includes a Bollywood-lesson intermission

- Main characters who are regular people who turned out to have a royal pedigree

- Movies that pivot around a road trip that changes a person's life

- Beach-themed movies

Stove-Top Popcorn

MAKES ABOUT 12 CUPS

3 tablespoons oil with a
high smoke point, such as canola,
grapeseed, coconut, peanut,
or melted duck or bacon fat

⅔ cup popcorn kernels

Toppings (suggestions follow)

Stove-top popcorn is a must-have for your movie night. Serve in classic concession boxes or large paper cones. There is a vast array of different corn kernel varieties available, including white, blue, red, and yellow; even hull-less options to avoid the pesky bits that lodge between teeth.

In a heavy-bottom, high-sided pot with a lid over medium-high heat, warm the oil and 3 popcorn kernels. Once a kernel pops, remove the pot from the heat, carefully add the rest of the kernels, cover the pot, and shake vigorously. Set the pot over medium heat and let the kernels pop while shaking the pot gently. When there are 4 to 5 seconds between each pop, remove the lid and tip the popcorn into a large bowl. Toss with your preferred toppings. Serve immediately.

POPCORN TOPPING IDEAS

- Pesto: combine 2 tablespoons grated Parmesan cheese with 1 teaspoon each garlic powder and dried basil

- Japanese: add 1 tablespoon furikake, which is a combination of sesame seeds, bonito, and dried seaweed (available at Asian specialty markets)

- Mexican: whisk together 1 tablespoon favorite hot sauce and 1 teaspoon each smoked paprika, dried oregano, toasted cumin powder, and onion flakes

- Indulge: stir together ¼ cup melted dark chocolate, 2 tablespoons finely chopped smoked almonds, and 1 teaspoon flaky sea salt; drizzle over your popcorn

- Bollywood: combine 1 tablespoon dried coconut flakes, juice of ½ lime, and 2 teaspoons toasted garam masala

- Scandinavian: stir together 2 tablespoons melted butter, 1 tablespoon freshly squeezed lemon juice, and 1 teaspoon each dried dill and onion powder

Hot Chocolate

SERVES 4

Nothing says "family time" at the end of a long day of outdoor activities like a cup of hot chocolate, especially on a chilly fall or winter afternoon. This incarnation of the ubiquitous childhood favorite is thick and rich, with butter to give it extra heft and salt to heighten the flavor. Freshly whipped cream is always our first choice, but store-bought works in a pinch. Use your best chocolate (such as Lindt, Ghirardelli, Green & Black's, Godiva, Valrhona, or Ritter) and whole milk for complete indulgence. For adults who need something extra after all the heavy snowman body-part lifting, add a splash of bourbon or Grand Marnier.

4 cups whole milk

10 ounces 50% (or higher) cacao chocolate, broken into 1-inch pieces

3 tablespoons unsalted butter

Pinch of kosher salt

Freshly whipped sweetened cream for serving

In a medium pot over medium-high heat, bring the milk to a simmer, being careful not to let it boil. Turn the heat to medium-low and add the chocolate and butter. Gently whisk continuously until the chocolate is melted and everything is fully incorporated. Sprinkle with the salt and pour into four mugs. Add a generous spoonful of whipped cream before serving.

DATE NIGHT

A romantic evening doesn't have to be an elaborate affair requiring meticulous planning. A night in, with a homemade meal next to a crackling fire when the wind is howling outside, is the hyggeligt way to date night. Prepare an easy meal that requires little fuss and includes dessert. Dim the lights, light enough candles to make the entire room sparkle, line the sofa with cushy blankets, and turn on a mellow playlist that has a song or two for dancing. Pour wine into polished glasses that glisten in the candlelight, relax, and enjoy. For a little extra coziness, handwrite your loved one a letter explaining why you love him or her, to be read while you're plating up the dinners. It's the hyggeligt way to a loved one's heart.

EASY GATHERINGS AND HOLIDAYS

Hosting a gathering, small or large, forges alliances that endure long after the party has ended. It reminds us that there is joy to be found in togetherness, compassion, and kindness.

Entertaining in a hyggeligt way focuses on the well-being of the people gathered together. It is not about luxurious dinners or extravagant decor. It's simple, stress-free engagement; it enables both host and guest to enjoy their time together, and guests to depart feeling better than when they arrived.

In wintertime, candles are always flickering at a hygge-fest, and good music is always playing in the background. Recipes are simple and comforting rather than elaborate, and there's not a cocktail dress in sight. Blankets and pillows are strewn about the place, and sometimes there are musical instruments, birch twig swizzle sticks, and ice skates.

Game nights, book clubs, knitting circles, and cocktail and pizza parties are all ways to bring people together for a giant slice of hygge-pie during the colder months. Outdoor entertaining around a bonfire, venturing into the snowy forest on snowshoes, and then gathering for a Thermos of soup and a snow-chilled beer—these are all ways to entertain with hygge style.

Springtime entertaining in Scandinavia reflects the time of renewal and awakening. Tabletops are festive, featuring an abundance of fresh flowers and colorful candles. There's always roast lamb and fruit pie on the menu.

Much of Scandinavian summertime entertaining takes place outside, to soak up as much sunshine as possible. Barbecues are popular ways to indulge a crowd. In Denmark and throughout most of Scandinavia, terrace gatherings around a grill, with chilled beer in hand and someone playing a guitar in the corner, tend to start during the late afternoon and conclude late in the evening when the midnight sun has not even thought about setting yet.

Autumn entertaining is the reason tents are embraced in Scandinavia. There's no better time to venture out into the forest for a camping party with friends than when the trees are ablaze with red, yellow, and orange. A cooler stocked with cold beverages; a pasta salad; sandwich fixings like lunch meat, cheese, pickles, and mustard; and a batch of freshly baked cookies make the perfect meal to tuck into around a campfire, surrounded by loved ones and backlit by fall's glorious colors.

There's always time for entertaining in Scandinavia, no matter the season. When it's at its hygge best, it includes laughter, music, simple food, and an abundance of good cheer.

THE PARTING GIFT

When you host an afternoon tea, a welcoming brunch, or a dinner filled with effervescent conversation, you amply demonstrate how much you care for your guests. But there's one more unexpected gesture you can make. Hostess gifts from guests are common, but a parting gift from host to guest is the ultimate hyggeligt gesture of love and gratitude. Your farewell token could be something edible, such as a loaf of bread like the one you all enjoyed during the meal, a jar of homemade jam or pickles (like the rhubarb pickles on page 148) in a decorative jar with a ribbon wrapped around it, or a nicely assembled tin of leftovers that your guest can enjoy the next day. A nonedible gift could be a book that you hope will inspire your guest, with a handwritten note on the frontispiece; herbs in an ornamental pot; or a candle with a fragrant aroma.

AROMATIC SUGAR

Aromatic sugar is an exquisite parting gift that is relatively inexpensive and easy to produce. Guests will appreciate your unexpected gesture and find endless uses for something that smells as lovely as it tastes. It is a lasting reminder of a lovely time spent together because sugar is a natural preservative. And it will be enjoyed by all ages, including those who appreciate a little pampering—many varieties can also be used as a bath scrub.

- Begin with a clean jar. Jam jars with lids work well, but glass storage jars with locking lids are even better since the seal is airtight.

- Granulated sugar is ideal because as long as it is kept dry, it will not clump like brown sugars tend to do.

- The aromatic is limited only by your imagination. A few ideas include culinary lavender, violet or rose petals, mint or basil leaves, cardamom or vanilla pods, coffee beans, chamomile, cinnamon sticks, or dried orange, lemon, or grapefruit peelings. For a Scandinavian flourish, try lemon balm leaves, arctic thyme, angelica blossoms, or juniper.

- Layer the ingredients in the jar, alternating between the sugar and your choice of aromatic. Then, seal the jar. That's it!

- For something extra-special, wrap the jar with a tea towel, cloth napkin, or swatch of fabric tied with a decorative ribbon. Attach a tag that identifies what kind of sugar it is (on the front), along with handwritten usage suggestions (on the back), such as rimming a martini glass, adding to coffee, sprinkling over muffins or scones before baking, or, if the aromatics are appropriate, using as a bath scrub.

Red Beet Salad with Hazelnuts, Pickled Onion, and Goat Cheese

SERVES 4

3 large red beets, rinsed thoroughly and peeled

Olive oil for drizzling

Kosher salt

One 12-ounce bottle pale ale

1 cup apple cider vinegar, plus more as needed

3 tablespoons granulated sugar

1 medium white onion, peeled, halved, and thinly sliced

1 cup cherry, cranberry, or pomegranate juice

2 tablespoons packed brown sugar

½ cup hazelnuts

2 tablespoons butter

Mesclun, baby spinach, arugula, or other greens for serving

Goat cheese, broken into pieces, for garnish

Sumac for garnish (optional)

This easily executed salad (most of the prep time is for beet roasting) is a festive way to kick off a holiday meal. The original recipe calls for homemade cheese but goat cheese—or blue cheese for a bit more funk—is a quick and easy substitute. Walnuts or sunflower seeds are good alternatives to hazelnuts; adjust the baking time accordingly. Be sure to wear plastic gloves when peeling the beets; beet-tinted hands might not be the kind of red you're looking for during the holidays. A powder made from dehydrated red beets is used as a garnish. The tangy Middle Eastern herb sumac would make a good substitute.

Preheat the oven to 325°F.

Drizzle the beets with olive oil and season with salt. Wrap each beet separately in a double layer of aluminum foil and bake until fork-tender, about 1 hour and 45 minutes. Once the beets are cool enough to handle, wearing disposable rubber or plastic kitchen gloves, cut them into irregular, bite-size pieces.

In a small pot over high heat, bring the ale, ½ cup of the cider vinegar, and 2 tablespoons of the granulated sugar to a vigorous simmer. Turn the heat to medium-low and cook the pickling liquid until the sugar is dissolved.

Place the onion in a medium bowl and pour the pickling liquid over it. Set aside at room temperature for 1 hour. Drain the onion and discard the pickling liquid.

In a small pot over medium-high heat, combine the remaining ½ cup vinegar, the cherry juice, and brown sugar and bring to a vigorous simmer. Continue to simmer until the mixture is a thin, syrupy consistency, about 30 minutes, stirring occasionally with a wooden spoon to prevent scorching. Set aside.

continued

Red Beet Salad with Hazelnuts, Pickled Onion, and Goat Cheese

Preheat the oven to 350°F.

On a baking sheet lined with aluminum foil, toss together the hazelnuts and remaining 1 tablespoon granulated sugar and then dot with the butter and season with salt and vinegar. Bake for 12 minutes, stirring once halfway through the baking time. Set aside. (The nuts will keep in an airtight container at room temperature for up to 3 days.)

Toss the beets with the cherry syrup until well coated. Season with salt.

Place a bed of greens on each of four salad plates and top with some of the beets, pickled onion, and hazelnuts. Garnish with goat cheese and sumac, if desired, before serving.

Baked Cod with Celeriac Puree, Chorizo, and Caramelized Onions

SERVES 4

1 cup whole milk

1 medium celeriac or 4 medium parsnips, peeled and coarsely chopped

1 Granny Smith apple, peeled, seeded, and coarsely chopped

Apple cider vinegar for seasoning, plus ¾ cup

Kosher salt

8 tablespoons butter

Four 8-ounce fresh cod fillets, skinned and deboned

1 medium white onion, halved and thinly sliced

1 cup chicken stock

Bacalao, dried salted cod, is a mainstay in many Scandinavian countries. It typically requires seven to nine months to preserve properly, which makes it an ideal food for winter when ingredients are scarce and the churning ocean too turbulent for fishing. (I call for fresh cod fillets here; if you do have access to bacalao, it's delightful, but cut back on the salt accordingly.) Brown butter is simply butter sautéed in a pan until it turns golden. Substitute parsnips for the celeriac for a sweeter flavor, and if you're looking for less heat, opt for a milder sausage variety.

In a medium saucepan over medium-high heat, bring the milk to a gentle simmer, being careful not to let it boil. Turn the heat to medium, add the celeriac, and simmer until fork-tender, about 30 minutes. Add half the chopped apple, then carefully transfer to a countertop blender (or use an immersion blender) and puree until smooth. Season with vinegar and salt and keep warm.

Preheat the oven to 350°F and line a baking dish with aluminum foil.

In a nonstick skillet over medium heat, melt 6 tablespoons of the butter until it begins to bubble and turns golden brown.

Salt the cod on both sides and then, using a pastry brush, brush each side with the brown butter (there will be some butter left over; set aside). Transfer the cod to the prepared baking dish and bake until cooked through, 9 to 11 minutes.

continued

Baked Cod with Celeriac Puree, Chorizo, and Caramelized Onions

4 ounces chorizo, thinly sliced and sautéed until crispy

Finely chopped toasted hazelnuts for garnish

Finely chopped herbs such as parsley, tarragon, or lemon verbena for garnish (optional)

In a small pot over medium heat, melt the remaining 2 tablespoons butter. Add the onion and sauté until tender. Add the ¾ cup vinegar and cook until reduced by half. Add the chicken stock and cook until reduced by half. Season with salt.

Place a spoonful of the celeriac puree on a plate and top with a cod fillet. Spoon the onion over the cod. Garnish with the chorizo, hazelnuts, remaining apple, and herbs, if desired. Drizzle with the remaining brown butter before serving.

Blackened Salmon with Cottage Cheese and Cider Vinaigrette

SERVES 6

2 tablespoons cumin seeds

2 tablespoons coriander seeds

2 tablespoons paprika

Six 8-ounce salmon steaks

Kosher salt

12 scallions, cut into
1-inch segments

1½ cups cottage cheese

⅔ cup apple cider vinegar

6 tablespoons canola oil

This recipe is a dynamic duo of elegant and easy. It's a lovely way to kick off a cocktail party, with minimal time required in the kitchen. The cottage cheese and cider vinaigrette can be made the day before, leaving nothing but frying the salmon and plating the dish on the day of the festivities. If you prefer a little less splattering and mess, instead of frying the salmon, bake at 350°F until just cooked through, 9 to 11 minutes. For a little extra flair, garnish with toasted pumpkin seeds and fresh dill.

In a small bowl, stir together the cumin, coriander, and paprika and transfer to a dinner plate, shaking the plate to evenly distribute.

Season the salmon steaks on both sides with salt. Dredge both sides of the salmon in the spice mix, pressing firmly to ensure that the spices adhere to the flesh.

Warm a cast-iron pan over high heat until nearly smoking. Add two of the steaks and fry until they are blackened and cooked through, approximately 4 minutes per side. Transfer to a plate to rest, then flip after 2 or 3 minutes to evenly distribute their cooking juices. Repeat the process with the remaining steaks. Add the scallions to the pan and quickly sauté until blackened.

In a bowl, gently stir together the cottage cheese and ½ cup of the vinegar until blended but still lumpy. Season with salt. In a small bowl, whisk together the remaining vinegar and the canola oil to make a vinaigrette.

Place each salmon steak on a dinner plate and top with a spoonful of the cottage cheese. Garnish with the blackened scallions and drizzle with the vinaigrette before serving.

Lamb Stew

SERVES 6

3 tablespoons canola oil

1 pound lamb loin, cut into 2-inch pieces

Kosher salt

Water, as needed

½ cup pearl barley

1 medium onion, coarsely chopped

2 medium leeks, white and pale green parts only, rinsed thoroughly and thinly sliced

2 medium carrots, peeled and coarsely chopped

½ small rutabaga, peeled and coarsely chopped

3 red potatoes, peeled and coarsely chopped

½ head green cabbage, cored and coarsely chopped

4 garlic cloves, finely chopped

6 thyme sprigs, leaves picked and twigs discarded

1 rosemary sprig, finely chopped

4 parsley sprigs, finely chopped

2 bay leaves

Sour cream, softened butter, and crusty bread for serving

This is the perfect dish to serve to a game-night crowd, especially during the winter. Icelanders have over a thousand years of experience in countering inclement weather, and we invite you to try one of their best defenses: *kjötsúpa* ("kyote-soo-pah"), or lamb stew. Steaming bowls of it are available in every home and restaurant throughout the nation during the winter, ladled from bubbling pots, aromatic with herbs and comfort. This is a wonderful dish for a crowd because it can be made ahead of time and served communally from the pot it was cooked in, fostering a sense of togetherness and ratcheting up the hygge with little effort from the cook. Angelica is commonly used in Iceland; in this recipe, the more readily available rosemary, parsley, and thyme are substituted. Carrots and parsnips are other nice winter additions. Serve with pints of IPA or red ale.

In a large, heavy-bottomed pot over high heat, warm the canola oil. Season the lamb with salt, add to the pot, and brown on all sides. Add enough water to cover the lamb by 6 inches and bring to a vigorous boil. Turn the heat to medium and gently simmer, partially covered, for 40 minutes. Add the barley and continue to simmer for another 40 minutes. Add the onion, leeks, carrots, rutabaga, potatoes, cabbage, garlic, thyme, rosemary, parsley, and bay leaves and simmer until the vegetables are tender, about 30 minutes more.

Place a bowl of sour cream on the table alongside a plate of softened butter and a loaf of crusty bread. Remove the bay leaves, transfer the pot to the table, and serve the stew using a ladle and enough soup bowls for everyone gathered around.

Braised Lamb Shanks with Bok Choy and Sweet-and-Sour Dill Oil

SERVES 6

Two 1-pound lamb shanks

Kosher salt

⅔ cup canola oil

½ cup apple cider vinegar

1 small onion, coarsely chopped

4 garlic cloves, thinly sliced

3 cups beef stock

¼ bunch dill

1 tablespoon granulated sugar

1 large bok choy, rinsed well and coarsely chopped

Don't let the long braising time in this recipe intimidate you. It's an easy "prepare it and forget about it" step and fills the house with a subtle enticing aroma that will make your guests' mouths water. It's a perfect company's-coming meal because it's guaranteed to impress. If you have leftovers, prepare open-faced lamb sandwiches by stacking a crusty slice of toasted bread with lettuce, red onions, and shredded lamb and drizzling with sweet-and-sour dill oil. The oil will keep in the refrigerator for up to 1 week, though it will lose a bit of its green luster over time.

Preheat the oven to 400°F. Have ready a large plate.

Season the lamb shanks with salt.

In an ovenproof pot with a tight-fitting lid over high heat, warm 2 tablespoons of the canola oil. Sear the lamb shanks on both sides until golden brown, about 2 minutes per side, then transfer to the plate.

Add 1 tablespoon of the vinegar to the pot and, using a wooden spoon, scrape up the brown bits at the bottom. Turn the heat to medium, add the onion and garlic, and sauté until the onion is translucent. Add the beef stock and remaining vinegar and bring to a simmer.

Return the shanks to the pot and press down to submerge them. Cover the pot, transfer to the oven, and braise the shanks until the meat is falling from the bone, about 1 hour and 45 minutes.

In a blender, combine the remaining canola oil, dill, and sugar and puree until smooth. Strain through a cheesecloth-lined fine-mesh sieve and transfer to a squeeze bottle.

continued

Braised Lamb Shanks with Bok Choy and Sweet-and-Sour Dill Oil

Remove the shanks from the pot and reserve the cooking liquid separately. Let the shanks cool, then return the liquid to medium-high heat. Simmer, stirring occasionally, until reduced to a thick, glossy sauce. Once the shanks are cool enough to handle, gently remove the meat from the bone.

Add the lamb meat and bok choy to the cooking liquid and stir until the bok choy is tender and the leaves are bright green, about 4 minutes. Season with salt. Spoon the lamb, bok choy, and sauce onto a serving platter and then drizzle with dill oil before serving.

Grilled Rib-Eyes with Herb Butter and Capers

Beef is a splurge in most Scandinavian homes, but sometimes steak is just the thing to serve at a cozy nighttime gathering. An indoor grill is key unless it's warm enough to fire up the one outside. Be sure to ask your guests how they prefer their steak; the hygge mood suffers when you deliver a well-done steak to the person who prefers it medium-rare. When selecting your steaks at the butcher, look for a bright red color, abundant marbling with streaks of fat running through the meat for even flavor distribution, and a good-size fat nugget nestled into the "eye." To keep it simple, set out bowls of capers and chopped parsley, but top the rested steaks with the herb butter yourself so it has time to melt down into the meat before it is served. Sprinkle with good crunchy sea salt and freshly ground black pepper, and don't forget the napkins—this dish, with its juices and melted butter, encourages sticky fingers.

SERVES 6

Six 1½-inch-thick aged rib-eye steaks

2 cups chilled butter, coarsely chopped

3 tablespoons capers

Leaves of 6 parsley sprigs, coarsely chopped

Apple cider vinegar for seasoning

Sea salt

Canola oil for drizzling

Finely chopped herbs such as parsley, tarragon, or chives for garnish (optional)

Let the steaks rest at room temperature for 20 minutes.

In a saucepan over medium-high heat, warm 1 cup of the butter until it begins to turn golden brown. Remove the pan from the heat and let cool to room temperature.

Add the remaining 1 cup butter to a blender and blend on high speed until it is light and fluffy. Add the brown butter and blend on medium speed until fluffy.

Using a spatula, transfer the whipped butter to a medium bowl. Fold in the capers and half the parsley and season with vinegar and salt. Transfer to a serving bowl, cover with plastic wrap, and refrigerate until ready to use.

continued

Grilled Rib-Eyes with Herb Butter and Capers

Prepare an indoor grill to high heat and oil the grate.

Season all sides of the steaks with salt and drizzle with canola oil. Grill each steak to the requested doneness (see Note), flipping once during the grilling process.

Once your steaks have reached your guest's desired doneness, let rest for 10 minutes, flipping after 5 minutes to evenly distribute their juices. Top each steak with a generous spoonful of chilled fluffed butter and garnish with herbs, if desired, before serving.

Note: Steak becomes firmer as it cooks, so the firmer the steak, the more well done it is. Here's a handy test: Make a circle with your thumb and *index* finger and push into the fleshy part of your palm below your thumb with the index finger of your other hand. A rare steak will feel similar. Make a circle with your thumb and *middle* finger and press the same area. This is how a medium-rare steak will feel. Now make a circle with your thumb and *ring* finger and press again. This is how a medium steak will feel. Now make a circle with, you guessed it, your *pinky* finger and thumb, and press again. That's a well-done steak.

A HYGGE PIZZA PARTY

Scandinavians love pizza as much as anyone else on the planet. They've found a way to make it their own by adding Nordic toppings that tend to be healthier than the extravagant U.S. incarnations. A hygge kind of pizza party invites guests of all ages to do the work, because in this case, the heavy lifting is convivial and fun.

Most grocery stores carry premade pizza dough. This makes it easy for the host, who can then focus on pulling together a variety of unique toppings. Plan to have one ball of pizza dough per person, so guests can personalize their pie. Provide bowls of flour for dusting, and encourage everyone to roll out the dough as thinly as possible so it turns crispy when baked.

Turn on some buoyant music and break out the wine, beer, and natural sodas to set the hygge tone. Place two pizza stones in the oven and crank it up to its highest temperature. This will ensure a crispy crust. If you don't have a stone, substitute a preheated baking sheet to achieve a similar result.

Arrange bowls of toppings on a large table. Some Scandinavian favorites include sunflower and pumpkin seeds, hazelnuts, arugula, smoked lamb, dill, fresh wild mushrooms, thinly sliced boiled potatoes, capers, figs, thinly sliced shallots, and a variety of cheeses.

Place small bowls of snacks, like sugared almonds and high-quality olives, here and there for guests to munch on while they work.

If you have a pizza peel or paddle, by all means put it to work; if not, simply use a sturdy oven mitt to transfer the stones in and out of the oven. When the pies are done, assign one person to slicing duty, and place a bowl of garlic aioli on the table to use for dipping, along with chili flakes for people who prefer a little more heat.

GAME NIGHT

Hosting a successful hygge game night is about setting the scene. You will need to decide on a theme and offer a variety of appealing games. When selecting games, be sensitive to the ages and skills of each of your guests. Have plenty of snacks available that don't require more than one hand to consume. Snacks should be tidy and easy to handle in order to prevent game interference, sticky dice or cards, or excessive crumbs.

Setting the Scene

- Light candles, place a cozy blanket on each chair, and arrange the chairs evenly around the table. Be sure to leave enough space on the table for the game, each player's game pieces, and a small plate and glass at each setting. If you are sitting on the floor, arrange fluffy pillows and throws around the table.

- Don't dive into games right away. Between arrival and getting down to business, leave at least an hour that can be filled with snacks and conversation. Play music during this time to set the mood.

- Understand the rules of each game you are offering and explain these before you begin.

- If tabulation is required during the game, ask for a volunteer ahead of time.

- If you are offering alcoholic beverages, don't serve anything stronger than light beer or wine in order to keep minds sharp and alert.

Game Night Themes

- Scandinavian: *Hnefatafl*—this is one of the oldest games in the world, is not language dependant, and is referred to as "The Viking Game" or "The King's Table." It was the game of noble Scandinavians and has Welsh, Celtic, and Saxon roots.

- Classics: Pictionary, Clue, Risk, Trivial Pursuit, Monopoly

- Strategy: Settlers of Catan, Mage Night, Ticket to Ride, Euphoria, Dominion

- Teamwork: Legends of Andor, Samurai Spirit, Forbidden Island, Castle Panic

- Dice Games: Qwixx, Liar's Dice, Roll for the Galaxy, Yahtzee, Blueprints

Snacks

- Hummus or white bean dip with baked pita triangles and vegetables, such as baby carrots and bell pepper strips

- Flavored popcorn (see page 69)

- Soft pretzel bites with honey-mustard dipping sauce

- Mozzarella, basil, and cherry tomato skewers

- Teriyaki chicken skewers with a peanut dipping sauce

- Middle Eastern feta and spinach spanakopita with a roasted red pepper dip

- Chicken bites sprinkled with dry cheese and chile flakes before baking

- Icelandic cookies (see pages 105 and 107)

COOKIE PARTY

Who doesn't love a good cookie party? For children, there is no treat like licking the spoon during an afternoon baking session. Store-bought or bakery-made holiday goodies work in a pinch, but try to set aside an evening to bake, get messy, and share stories with your children about your own holiday cookie times when you were a kid. Offer a variety of icings in different colors; add different aromatics (such as vanilla, cinnamon, and orange zest) to the dough, and by all means, let there be sprinkles. Crank up the festive music, dance while the cookies are in the oven, light candles with a spiced aroma, and fill the house with hygge-cheer. Try the ginger cookies on page 109, the kökur on page 105, or the kleinur on page 17.

Meringue Buttons

MAKES APPROXIMATELY 48 BUTTONS

3 egg whites

⅔ cup granulated sugar

Seeds from ½ vanilla pod
or 1½ teaspoons vanilla extract

5 ounces unsweetened
corn flakes

3½ ounces unsweetened
shredded coconut

4½ ounces dark chocolate,
coarsely chopped

¼ teaspoon kosher salt

These meringue buttons are simple to execute and just as fun for adults as they are for kids. The crunchy texture of the corn flakes is a satisfying contrast to the airy meringue.

Preheat the oven to 300°F and line a baking sheet with parchment paper.

In a large, chilled metal bowl, whisk together the egg whites, sugar, and vanilla until a meringue with stiff peaks forms. Alternatively, use a stand mixer fitted with a whisk attachment.

In a large bowl, stir together the corn flakes, coconut, chocolate, and salt.

Using a spatula, gently stir the cornflake mixture into the meringue until just incorporated. Then, evenly distribute in 1-tablespoon-size buttons, about 1 inch apart, on the prepared baking sheet.

Bake until the meringues are cooked through, 12 to 15 minutes. Let cool to room temperature, then remove from the baking sheet. The buttons will keep in a covered container, separated with layers of parchment paper, at room temperature for up to 3 days.

Kökur
(Icelandic Cookies)

MAKES APPROXIMATELY
30 KÖKUR

1¼ cups all-purpose flour,
plus more for rolling

⅓ cup granulated sugar

7 tablespoons butter,
at room temperature

1 egg

1 to 2 teaspoons cold water

Sea salt

One 8-ounce bar high-quality
chocolate (licorice flavored,
if desired), finely grated

Kökur ("koo-ker") means "cake" in Icelandic, and these tiny beauties are a sweet and lovely finish to a holiday meal. They're also a family favorite because they are so simple—they take no time at all. Gunnar's son Mikael has been cooking at his father's side since he was a tiny tot, and these are a father-son favorite to make together. Crunchy sea salt and chocolate shavings give the cookies unexpected texture and a sophisticated finish. This recipe originally called for licorice chocolate, a flavor combination beloved throughout Scandinavia. If this appeals to you and you have access to it, by all means try it. Otherwise, any high-quality chocolate will do. Serve with a glass of ice-cold milk.

Preheat the oven to 300°F and line a baking sheet with parchment paper.

In a medium bowl, stir together the flour and sugar until well blended. Add the butter and egg and mix with your hands until a ball of shaggy dough forms. If the dough feels too dry and does not hold together, add the water.

Sprinkle a thin layer of flour onto a clean work surface and, using a rolling pin, roll out the dough about ½ inch thick. Using a 2-inch round cutter, cut out circles and transfer to the prepared baking sheet. Gather up the dough scraps, roll out into another layer, and continue forming cookies until all of the dough has been used. Lightly sprinkle the cookies with sea salt.

Bake until the cookies are crispy, about 15 minutes. While the cookies are still warm, sprinkle the grated chocolate over half of them and top each with one of the remaining cookies to form a cookie sandwich. Let cool to room temperature. The cookies will keep in a covered container at room temperature for up to 3 days.

Ástarpungar
(Love Balls)

MAKES APPROXIMATELY
30 ÁSTARPUNGAR

2½ cups all-purpose flour
½ cup granulated sugar
2 teaspoons baking powder
1 egg
1½ cups cultured buttermilk
3 tablespoons golden raisins
1 gallon canola oil
Confectioners' sugar for dusting
(optional)

Ástarpungar ("est-ar-pun-ger"), nicknamed "love balls," are fried balls of dough still served on a weekly basis in some Icelandic households, and nearly every Icelander has a memory of eating them with a cold glass of milk as a child. Don't worry about a perfect shape when you're frying them; it's their irregularity that makes them fun, and their crispy golden skins and airy centers that make them addictive.

In a large bowl, sift together the flour, granulated sugar, and baking powder. Stir in the egg. Add the buttermilk in increments until the mixture forms a wet batter that is not runny; a spoonful should hold its shape without running off the spoon. Stir in the raisins.

In a heavy-bottomed pot, heat the canola oil to 350°F. Prepare a plate with a double layer of paper towels.

Working in batches, being careful not to crowd the pot and letting the oil heat back up between batches, scoop up about 2 tablespoons of batter with a spoon and use a second spoon to carefully push the batter into the oil. The batter will initially sink, but after about 4 minutes it should rise to the surface and begin to turn golden. Flip it over when the underside begins to turn golden and fry for about 1 minute more.

Using a slotted spoon, transfer the ástarpungar to the prepared plate to drain. Dust with confectioners' sugar, if desired, and serve piping hot.

Orange and Chocolate Cookies

MAKES APPROXIMATELY
25 COOKIES

2¼ cups all-purpose flour

½ cup granulated sugar

½ cup packed brown sugar

½ teaspoon baking soda

1 teaspoon baking powder

Zest and juice of 2 navel oranges; zest grated using a Microplane, juice simmered until reduced by half

¾ cup plus 1 tablespoon butter, at room temperature

2 eggs

One 8-ounce high-quality chocolate bar, broken into approximately 1-inch squares

The flavors of orange and chocolate are brilliant hygge-cookie partners. The citrus brightens the taste, transforms humdrum cookie brown into autumn orange, and is an excellent way to sneak a daily dose of vitamin C into the diet. Mandarins are an elegant substitute for navel oranges. For a bit of pucker, swap out half the orange zest and juice with lemon or even lime. Serve the cookies hot from the oven, while the gooey melted chocolate is at its very best, with a glass of ice-cold milk.

In a large bowl, combine the flour, granulated sugar, brown sugar, baking soda, baking powder, and orange zest and stir to incorporate. Add the butter, eggs, and orange juice and stir until incorporated and the dough forms a shaggy ball. Cover the dough with a damp cloth towel and refrigerate until chilled.

Preheat the oven to 325°F.

Form 1-tablespoon-size pieces of dough into balls by rolling between your palms. Arrange the balls on an ungreased baking sheet, leaving about 1½ inches between them. Gently press a piece of chocolate into the center of each ball until the ball is approximately ¾ inch thick.

Bake until the cookies are golden brown, 8 to 10 minutes. Let cool to room temperature, then remove from the baking sheet. The cookies will keep in a covered container at room temperature for up to 4 days.

Ginger Cookies

MAKES APPROXIMATELY
36 COOKIES

2 cups all-purpose flour

2 cups packed brown sugar

4 teaspoons baking powder

½ teaspoon baking soda

1 teaspoon ground ginger

½ teaspoon ground cinnamon

¼ teaspoon ground cloves

½ cup melted butter

1 egg

These dainty cookies are a snacker's delight, with their spicy finish and addictive crunch, and just made for dunking in hot chocolate or ice-cold milk. They're also perfect for family time, because the dough can be made ahead, wrapped in plastic wrap, and refrigerated for up to three days, until you're ready to bake. Get the whole family involved in rolling out the dough and cutting the circles.

In a large bowl, sift together the flour, brown sugar, baking powder, baking soda, ginger, cinnamon, and cloves. Add the butter and egg and stir with a wooden spoon until the batter comes together to form a moist, malleable dough. Roll the dough into a 2-inch-diameter cylinder, wrap in plastic wrap, and refrigerate until well chilled.

Preheat the oven to 350°F and line a baking sheet with parchment paper.

Slice the chilled dough approximately ½ inch thick and arrange the slices 1 inch apart on the prepared baking sheet.

Bake until the cookies are crispy, 5 to 7 minutes. Transfer to a wire rack and let cool to room temperature. The cookies will keep in a covered container at room temperature for up to 1 week.

Laufabrauð

No other pastry in Iceland embodies the holidays more joyfully than *laufabrauð* ("lawf-a-brode"), or "leaf bread." Adults throughout the nation can share childhood stories of making these pretty little pastries with their family, just as they now make them with their own children and grandchildren. The cutting tools, called *laufabrauðsjárn*, are family heirlooms, passed down from one generation to the next. You can buy them online or at Scandinavian specialty shops; the Icelandic company Nammi ships worldwide. Each one, in its delicate spinning wheel, conjures cherished family memories of holidays made all the more festive by these special delicacies. Traditionally, laufabrauð are large round circles similar to flatbread, with designs made internally. Gunnar prepares his by cutting out parallelograms with decorative edges using the laufabrauðsjárn. If you can't find a laufabrauðsjárn, a paring knife will do. These are best served warm right after they've been fried, preferably with a group of good friends or family at the table, with glasses of cold milk.

MAKES APPROXIMATELY 48 SMALL PASTRIES

1½ cups whole milk

½ cup water

6 tablespoons butter

7¼ cups all-purpose flour, plus more for rolling

5 tablespoons granulated sugar

1 teaspoon baking powder

½ teaspoon baking soda

Kosher salt

Canola oil for frying

Ground cinnamon for sprinkling (optional)

In a saucepan over medium-high heat, bring the milk and water to a vigorous simmer. Add the butter and stir until it is melted and incorporated. Remove the pan from the heat.

In a large bowl, sift together the flour, sugar, baking powder, baking soda, and 1 teaspoon salt. Add the warm liquid to the bowl and stir with a wooden spoon to incorporate.

Sprinkle flour onto a clean work surface. Lightly oil a large bowl.

Turn out the dough onto the work surface, and knead until it springs back when poked with a finger. Transfer to the oiled bowl and cover with a damp cloth.

Working quickly, add more flour to your work surface, break off about one-third of the dough and, using a rolling pin, roll it out ¼-inch thick. Using your laufabrauðsjárn, cut straight lines in the dough from one side to the other and then, working in the opposite direction, cut out squares, diamonds, or rectangles about 1 inch by 2 inches or 1½ inches square. Place the damp cloth over the cut pieces and repeat the process with the remaining dough.

Pour about 2 inches of canola oil into a heavy-bottomed pot and heat to 250°F. Line a plate with a double layer of paper towels and place it next to the stove.

Working very quickly with dry fingers, carefully transfer several squares to the hot oil; don't overcrowd the pot. Fry the laufabrauð until they just start to turn golden brown, about 1 minute per side.

Using a spider or a slotted spoon, transfer the laufabrauð to the prepared plate to drain. Sprinkle with salt and cinnamon, if desired. Repeat the process with the remaining squares. The laufabrauð will keep in an airtight container, separated with layers of parchment paper, at room temperature for up to 3 days.

A COZY COCKTAIL PARTY

There's nothing like a rollicking cocktail party to bring all the grown-ups together on a gusty winter evening. Make it cozy with lively music, natural swizzle sticks such as tiny tree twigs, and plenty of easy-to-eat appetizers to soak up the alcohol. Encourage guests to get involved in the cocktail making; give a lively demo and share the history and interesting facts about the spirits or cocktails you're offering.

A gin gimlet is a refreshing springtime libation. In the summertime, give the classic mojito a Scandinavian twist by substituting vodka for the rum and adding an equal amount of fresh dill to the mint leaves. Autumn is the perfect season for hot spiked cider, complete with a cinnamon stick and freshly grated nutmeg. And in winter, there's nothing like the warming qualities of whiskey. Try a whiskey old-fashioned with a drizzle of maple syrup and a sprig of rosemary for a festive flourish.

No matter what the season, send each person home with a few cocktail recipes or, better yet, a small bottle of homemade syrup or bitters (see page 119).

The Tom Cat

MAKES 2 COCKTAILS

2 ounces Hayman's Old Tom gin

2 ounces mezcal

1½ ounces dry sherry

1½ ounces sweet vermouth (Antica is a good choice)

8 drops House Bitters (page 119)

Ice cubes

Dehydrated grapefruit slices for garnish

One endearing quality of hygge is its embrace of nostalgia and tradition. Vintage decor, retro clothing styles, and classic recipes are celebrated facets of a hygge lifestyle. This drink, inspired by a nineteenth-century British gin recipe, is an updated version of the original Old Tom gin cocktail, with the addition of mezcal from Mexico for smokiness, vermouth for sweetness, and bitters for complexity. Old Tom gin is appreciated by contemporary bartenders because it's considered a missing gin link, being a bit drier than Dutch jenever and a little sweeter than London Dry. It's available in most well-stocked liquor stores, but if you have trouble sourcing it, opt for a drier gin, since this recipe already includes a sweet spirit. This is a fantastically elegant cocktail—so be prepared, your guests will most likely request more than one.

In a cocktail shaker, combine the gin, mezcal, sherry, vermouth, and bitters. Add enough ice to fill the shaker to the top and shake vigorously. Strain into two coupe glasses, add a few large chunks of ice, and garnish with grapefruit slices before serving.

Birch Sour

Birch is commonly used throughout Scandinavia in food products such as syrups and jams. Recently, birch schnapps, liqueur, and vodka have emerged as spirit favorites in Iceland. Birch schnapps is difficult to come by outside of the country, so if you're fortunate enough to journey there, be sure to pick up a bottle before you head home. If you don't have access to it, a smoky whisky, such as Talisker from Scotland, works well; for something sweeter, try amaretto. The bitters are a nice counterpoint to the sugar syrup, while the egg white adds a frothy finish. This recipe makes more brown sugar syrup than you'll need for the cocktail; drizzle the extra over waffles, pancakes, or ice cream.

MAKES 1 COCKTAIL

Brown Sugar Syrup
½ cup packed brown sugar

½ cup water

1 egg white

2 ounces birch schnapps, smoky whisky such as Talisker, or amaretto

2 dashes House Bitters (page 119)

Ice cubes

Orange zest and a thyme sprig for garnish

To make the brown sugar syrup: In a small pot, combine the brown sugar and water and bring to a simmer over medium-high heat. Whisk until the sugar dissolves and the syrup is thick enough to coat the back of a wooden spoon. Let cool. The syrup will keep in a covered container in the refrigerator for up to 1 week.

In a cocktail shaker, combine the egg white, schnapps, 1 teaspoon of the brown sugar syrup, and the bitters. Shake vigorously until you feel the pressure begin to build inside the shaker as a result of the egg white expansion. Carefully release the seal, add enough ice to fill the shaker, seal once more, and shake vigorously for about 30 seconds.

Strain into a chilled coupe glass and garnish with orange zest and thyme before serving.

Glögg

SERVES 12

The spiced wine called *glögg* ("glug") is as synonymous with Scandinavian winter holidays as twinkling lights and snowflakes. The whole spices can be tossed together and toasted in a very dry pan over medium heat until they become aromatic. This version calls for white wine, which lightens it and allows the spices and other aromatics within to glisten and shine. It's a wonderful way to commence the merry-making.

Two 750-ml bottles dry white wine

1 cup vodka

½ cup granulated sugar

2 tablespoons honey

1 tablespoon vanilla extract

4 star anise pods, toasted

2 cinnamon sticks, toasted

6 cloves, toasted

6 cardamom pods, toasted

½ lemon, thinly sliced

½ orange, thinly sliced

½ cup blanched almonds, toasted

One 1-inch-long piece fresh ginger, peeled, sliced in half lengthwise, and crushed with the back of a spoon

In a large pot over medium heat, combine the wine, vodka, sugar, honey, and vanilla and bring to a gentle simmer. Turn the heat to medium-low; add the star anise, cinnamon, cloves, cardamom, lemon, orange, almonds, and ginger; and gently simmer for another 10 minutes, until aromatic and flavorful.

Transfer the glögg to a clear pitcher, where the aromatics will look festive and alluring. Serve hot in mugs or mulled wine glasses.

Berry Spritzers

This is a healthful and fun summer drink that the entire family will love. Fresh, ripe berries are plentiful during the warmer months, and a refreshing way to enjoy them is to transform them into this invigorating spritzer. Even if you don't have time to pick berries, store-bought juice without any additives (like corn syrup) works in a pinch. Blackberries, raspberries, strawberries, or blueberries all are tasty options, either on their own or as a mixture. A sprinkle of salt heightens the berry flavor.

MAKES 2 QUARTS (SERVES 8)

6 cups soda water

2 cups freshly squeezed or store-bought berry juice

3 tablespoons honey or agave nectar

Pinch of kosher salt

4 lime wedges

4 mint sprigs, plus more for garnish

Ice cubes

In a large glass pitcher, combine the soda water, berry juice, honey, and salt and stir with a wooden spoon to combine. Add the lime wedges and mint sprigs and stir once more. Refrigerate for about 30 minutes to give the flavors time to mingle. Serve over ice, garnished with mint sprigs.

House Bitters

This recipe might seem complicated but is worth the time since it will last for ages, as most cocktails that call for it require only a few drops to deliver extraordinary dividends. Bitters are typically made using the extraction of seeds and roots; this is an easier version requiring spices and aromatics that you most likely already have in your pantry. The trick is to give the ingredients time to mingle once they're combined, ideally for two to two and a half weeks. Gifting departing guests with the bitters in a tiny cobalt blue or amber bottle fitted with an eye-dropper lid is a lovely way to keep the spirit of the party with them even when they arrive back home. For a special touch, add a handmade label to each bottle with the name and bottling date. Recipes that call for these bitters are on pages 114 and 116. For sterilizing directions, see Note on page 148.

MAKES 1 QUART

Peels from 3 oranges and 2 grapefruits, pith scraped away with a paring knife, thinly sliced

Peel from 1 lemon, thinly sliced

2½ cups overproof rum (rum with an alcohol content greater than 57.5%)

2 cinnamon sticks

1 star anise pod

4 cardamom pods

¼ teaspoon freshly grated nutmeg

Preheat the oven to 225°F and line a baking sheet with parchment paper.

Arrange two-thirds of the orange peels and all of the grapefruit peels on the prepared baking sheet and bake until the peels are completely dehydrated, 25 to 30 minutes. Let cool to room temperature and then remove from the parchment paper.

In a large, sterilized glass jar fitted with a tight lid, combine the dehydrated peels with the lemon peel, rum, cinnamon, star anise, cardamom, and nutmeg. Shake vigorously and store in a warm, dry place near a window for 2 to 2½ weeks, or until the desired flavor intensity is achieved.

Transfer the liquid to a pot and bring to a simmer over medium heat. Simmer for 5 minutes and then let cool to room temperature. Strain through a fine-mesh sieve lined with a double layer of cheesecloth. Using a funnel, transfer the bitters to small bottles fitted with eye-droppers. The bitters will keep in a cool, dry place for up to 1 year.

ORNAMENTS

There's so much more to handmade ornaments than strings of popcorn and cranberries. And decorations crafted from felt, wood, yarn, and natural elements like pinecones and birch bark are highly valued in Scandinavian countries. This fun craft project for children and adults alike, if packed away with care at the end of the season, become heirlooms that happily re-emerge year after year.

For a simple ornament, stick toothpicks into soaked garbanzo beans to form triangles. Carefully place on a baking sheet and transfer to a gas oven warmed by its pilot light. Allow to dehydrate until the garbanzo beans are completely dried, 14 to 16 hours. Using red ribbon, tie two triangles together to form a star. Attach a red ribbon loop to each and hang them on the tree. Don't worry about making handcrafted ornaments perfect; their rustic nature is the essence of their charm.

Scandinavian Holidays and Their Traditions

Scandinavians live for the holidays. Fall and winter celebrations are a time for gratitude throughout the region. They are about gathering loved ones to share the reasons why those close to you are appreciated and to offer good wishes for the year to come. Spring and summertime holidays are festive occasions enjoyed outside under a cheery blue sky. You can create your own cozy hygge holidays for every season anywhere in the world. They don't require snow or reindeer, fireworks or bonfires—just people you love, recipes cooked long and slow, and thoughtful gifts filled with meaning. Don't fret over complicated details. Let them go. It's not the elaborate centerpiece guests will remember, but the way they felt gathered around your table. Wear comfy clothes for a hygge holiday, and don't forget to light the fire.

St. Knut's Day | January 13

St. Knut's Day is traditionally the date when seasonal merrymaking comes to an end. It originated in the Middle Ages with an association to the Danish King Canute (Knut) IV, who was martyred and eventually became the patron saint of Denmark. Before his death, each year he asked for assistance from the Danish Guilds, or trading companies, to "drive out Christmas," which brought the winter revelry to an end. The holiday is celebrated in both Sweden and Denmark, where citizens of larger cities traditionally tossed their trees to the sidewalk from windows and over balconies, the wood was collected and used for bonfires during Walpurgis Night (see page 126). Over time, this day came to be associated with children going door to door asking for the last of any Christmas cookies and candy; a wintertime version of Halloween. St. Knut's Day is a fading holiday, but for some it offers one last moment to savor holiday indulgences before the long winter closes in around them.

Thorrablot | Mid-January to Mid-February

Thorrablot is a midwinter feast celebrated throughout Iceland. Visitors from abroad might not enjoy this holiday's spread of traditional food items—such as *mysa* (soured milk), *hakarl* (putrefied

Greenland shark), sheep fat, jellied ham, smoked and pickled items such as lamb testicles and brains, and a caraway-spiked schnapps known as Brennivin—but for Icelanders, it's a way to connect to their past and honor the resiliency and creativity of their Viking ancestors. Those tenacious people created these food products to get through brutal winters and are remembered with respect and fondness at Thorrablot celebrations. In the countryside, Thorrablot gatherings include a buffet of these dishes along with plenty of Brennivin to wash it all down. Music and dancing kick off an evening of jubilation that often lasts long into the black Icelandic night.

Fastelavn/Shrovetide | 40 days before Easter

Shrovetide is celebrated by Scandinavian Christians in a similar way that Fat Tuesday is enjoyed in other parts of the world. Depending upon the nation, it is also referred to as Fastelavn, an Old Danish term that means "fast-evening." It was customarily a time when children went from door to door asking for money, which eventually evolved into receiving cream-filled buns and other sweets. Like Fat Tuesday, it takes place on the Tuesday before Ash Wednesday, which marks the period leading up to Easter that is associated with fasting and sacrifice, and includes lavish meals and debauchery. On this day, Shrovetide buns are available in bakeries throughout Scandinavia. Shrovetide rods, birch branches festooned with sweets and small gifts, adorn homes throughout the region. The rod originally represented fertility since the spring branches were filled with buds on the verge of blooming. In Iceland, where Shrovetide is referred to as *Bolludagur* and was introduced by Danish and Norwegian bakers, the holiday is especially fun for children. Each child routinely receives one cream puff for each tap of the *bolluvondur*, a specially made bun-paddle used exclusively during the holiday, to adult bums. When asked about the meaning behind this custom, the Icelandic chocolate-maker who explained it to us shrugged, grinned, and said, "Because it's fun."

Easter | The March Equinox

Easter has its origins in the ancient Nordic festival of Ostara, honoring the Goddess of Spring. It is a ritual of renewal and rejoicing. Colored eggs and rabbits, modern-day symbols of Easter, find their origins in Ostera. The eggs were offered as gifts symbolizing a wish for prosperity; rabbits represented fertility and rebirth. In Finland, contemporary Easter celebrations include braided *pulla* bread, sweet buns flavored with cardamom and sometimes almonds and raisins. In Sweden, crispy *olof* rolls are served with hard-boiled eggs. In Norway, Easter is all about oranges. On this holiday, Norwegians consume three times as many oranges, clementines, and tangerines than they do for the rest of the year. Throughout all of Scandinavia, eggs and lamb are the predominant ingredients found on virtually every Easter table.

Walpurgis Night | April 30

In Sweden and Finland, Walpurgis Night is celebrated on April 30. Traditionally a German holiday, Walpurgis is the feast day of Saint Walpurga. According to folkloric tradition, this was the night witches gathered in the Harz Mountains of Germany. The remaining vestiges of this ancient belief include wooden witches that decorate homes, and colorful hats and capes celebrants wear to mark the holiday. Nonalcoholic mead, called *sima* in Finnish, is served along with tiny doughnuts and funnel cakes. People also enjoy other festive foods and sparkling cider or wine on the day after Walpurgis Night, which is also Labor Day throughout most of Scandinavia.

Midsummer | Summer Solstice

Midsummer in late June, the longest day of the year, is celebrated with relish throughout all of Scandinavia. In the countryside, bonfires blaze at summer cottages, and in cities, outdoor sidewalk parties spill into the streets. Fireworks conclude an evening of collective entertaining throughout the entire region. Grilled lamb and beef are popular foods to serve alongside chilled wine, beer, and aquavit.

All Saints' Day | Early November

All Saints' Day is a Christian holiday intended to commemorate individuals, both known and unknown, who have been christened saints. It is also a day to honor deceased relatives. It shares its origins with Halloween, an evening of costumes and trick-or-treating that has lost much of its spiritual provenance. On All Saints' Day throughout Scandinavia, devout Christians typically visit the graves of their relatives, lighting candles and saying a prayer to honor and remember those who came before.

St. Martin's Day | November 11

Other than being a time when Scandinavians enjoy a roasted goose on their dinner table on November 10, Martinman Eve, most people have forgotten the origins of this unique holiday. Saint Martin was a Roman soldier who was in hiding to avoid his obligation to become a bishop. Geese revealed his location and in revenge, Martin supposedly ate them. Other associations with this holiday include it being when the harvest concluded in agrarian communities, commemorated with the slaughter of a fattened cow and a feast. This is where the term "Martinmas beef" originates. In some parts of Sweden, *svartsoppa* (blacksoup) comprising goose blood and spices, is eaten on St. Martin's Day.

St. Lucia's Day | December 13

St. Lucia's Day is a major celebration in Sweden where Lucia, who introduced Christianity to the nation and was martyred by the Romans in AD 304 because of her beliefs, is commemorated by young girls who dress in white robes and adorn their heads with wreaths encircled with glowing candles. Today, this holiday is enjoyed in most of Scandinavia as a day of hope and a festival of lights. Traditional foods such as saffron bread called *lussekatter* and ginger biscuits are offered to visitors and savored by observant families.

Christmas Eve and Christmas Day | December 24 and 25

Christmastime is big commercial and spiritual business throughout all of Scandinavia. What better place to observe the epitome of all winter holidays than in a region dominated by the ethereal gaslit glow of northern lights casting their flickering blue and green fingers across an endless expanse of pristine white snow? Christmas trees are festooned with fairy lights, and in Sweden, a dish called *risgryngrot*, a rice pudding with one almond hidden inside, is served on Christmas Eve. It is believed that the person who discovers the almond is destined for marriage in the year ahead. After the feast of a Christmas *smorgasbord*, or buffet, traditionally comprising dishes like pickled herring and red beet salad, gravlax, *kottbullar med potatismos* (meatballs with mashed potatoes), and plenty of spiced wine called *glögg* (see page 117), someone at the table dons the Tomte costume (a Christmas gnome who looks similar to Santa Claus) and hands out the gifts while reciting traditional holiday poetry. *Juletid* (Christmastime) in Norway includes the decorating of *pepperkakker* (gingerbread) that is cut into festive shapes using cookie cutters. After the cookies are decorated, a hole is fashioned near the top of each one, a ribbon is strung through it, and they are traditionally hung in windows and on trees until Christmas day. A Christmas dessert that few Danes could go without is *ris à l'amande*, a chilled vanilla rice pudding topped with freshly whipped cream, toasted almonds, and warm cherry sauce. *Lanttulaatikko* is a must on Finnish Christmas tables. This creamy, baked rutabaga casserole is seasoned with nutmeg, molasses, and ginger.

No Christmas in Iceland would be complete without the thirteen yule lads. Beginning thirteen days before Christmas, Icelandic children leave their shoes out on windowsills. Each evening, one of the yule lads leaves a treat such as candy or a small gift in the shoes for kids to discover in the morning. The lads are a curious bunch, with some being nicer and others being more mischievous. There's one who slams doors, one who licks spoons, one who harasses sheep, one who steals meat, and even one who makes away with scraps left behind in cooking pots. When Icelanders aren't trying to locate their stolen Christmas meat, they're indulging in delicacies like *hamborgarhryggur* (glazed

rack of lamb), *ptarmigan* (grouse fattened on herbs and berries), *hangikjöt* (smoked lamb), and *laufabrauð* (an Icelandic Christmas cookie, see page 110).

St. Stephen's Day (Boxing Day) | December 26
St. Stephen's Day, or Boxing Day, which is celebrated throughout much of Europe, is a time to relax with family and indulge in Christmas leftovers that are often transformed into salads, soups, sandwiches, and casseroles and enjoyed on picnics, weather permitting.

New Year's Eve | December 31
Christmas is typically spent in the company of close family throughout Scandinavia, but New Year's Eve is meant to be relished with friends. In Denmark, where cries of *"Godt Nytår!"* ring out when the clock announces the midnight hour, menu mainstays include baked cod, cured pork, and stewed kale followed by a marzipan ring cake washed down with champagne at midnight. Wherever you are in Scandinavia on New Year's Eve, it is certain that the evening will be celebrated like it is in every other corner of the world, with fireworks, a glass of champagne, well wishes, a wee bit of debauchery, and a well-timed kiss.

GETTING OUT
EASY FORAYS, ADVENTURES, AND IDEAS
FOR ENJOYING THE OUTDOORS

Creating a cozy environment at home goes hand in hand with fostering a sense of togetherness and ease when you venture beyond your front door. The hygge spirit is carried along and requires nourishment, whether you find yourself ensconced in wool socks in front of the fireplace or exploring a distant corner of our planet where temperatures are too high to wear wool and fireplaces are used for cooking a one-pot family meal over an open flame.

One way to take your hygge sensibility with you on the road is to plan ahead for the journey that awaits you. Thinking through not only the trip itself but the day or two before the adventure begins ensures a smooth transition free of anxious moments. Packing a well-planned, hardworking wardrobe and all of the other items you will need to avoid frustration in an unknown place will heighten the experience you are there to have and ensure memories of it are not marred by frustration.

Traveling with children can be as rewarding as it is overwhelming While there's no guarantee that your child's travel experience will unfold without incident, preplanning will help them transition into an unfamiliar world with excitement in their hearts instead of anxiety. It will also keep your panic switch turned off in order to focus on generating positive memories with your children, not aggravating ones.

Traveling isn't always about a plane or train ticket. It can also involve a road trip where the adventure begins through your car window the moment you leave your driveway. Prepare transportable foods ahead of time to present to a famished crew the moment hunger pangs strike. Picnics are an enjoyable road-trip feature; spreading a blanket over a field of grass beneath a vast blue sky to savor a simple meal of well-considered recipes is sure to leave an indelible mark.

Getting outside doesn't have to mean venturing far beyond your doorstep. Gardening is a rewarding project for everyone in the family, resulting in a bounty on your dinner table at the end of the season. Children enjoy gardening as much as their parents, especially if they are involved in thought-provoking projects that are as educational as they are fun. Preserving the overflow ingredients from your garden is a way to carry the sense of wonder derived from nurturing a seed into a vegetable into the winter months.

Outdoor entertaining in both the warmer and colder months is another way to get out of the house without journeying too far. With a little planning, a casual party composed of dear friends and a springtime breeze can be as rewarding for the host as it is for the guest. Bestowing visitors with an unexpected gift upon their departure is a way to express gratitude that they showed up for your open-sky party.

PICNICS

Even on a crisp fall day or an unusually warm winter day, a picnic gets us out into the fresh air we all crave when days are shorter and the weather less inviting. Picnics inspire an easy rapport with others in a cozy, makeshift outdoor room beneath the open sky, close to forest or water.

Here are a few tips for a successful, stress-free picnic.

- Start with fun finger foods, such as fresh vegetables and toasted pita squares with hummus or a roasted red pepper dip

- Pasta, potato, and ancient-grain salads (such as amaranth and quinoa) hold up well and are easy to pack

- Layer salad ingredients in jam jars to transport them and provide a wow factor when they are served

- Keep sliced bread, meat, cheese, and other sandwich fillings like quick radish pickles (see page 141) separated until serving, to avoid sogginess

- Give the meal a sweet finish with cookies or brownies

- Stay hydrated with a Thermos of homemade soda—combine seltzer with sliced limes, a tablespoon of honey, and an unexpected juice flavor like watermelon or mango

- Pack cloth napkins, recyclable or compostable utensils, an ice pack, hand wipes, and a trash bag to collect rubbish

- In spring or summer, bring along a small vase; when you arrive at your picnic site, ask the children in your group to collect wildflowers for an arrangement

- Carry binoculars for birdwatching and a deck of cards and a kite for entertainment

- Be sure to pack extra blankets for guests to pull around their shoulders if it's chilly

Warm Potato Salad

SERVES 6

24 small, waxy potatoes like fingerlings or red bliss, skin on

6 eggs

2 tablespoons butter

1 shallot, finely chopped

2 tablespoons capers

Leaves of 1 parsley sprig, finely chopped

1 tablespoon Dijon mustard (use stone-ground mustard if you prefer something less tangy)

Apple cider vinegar for seasoning

Sea salt

Potato salad is classic road-trip food because it's a hearty crowd-pleaser able to withstand a long journey. This recipe is served warm, so you will need a kitchen at your destination to prepare the eggs and melt the butter. Other than that, it comes together in a few easy minutes. To pack this salad for the road, boil the potatoes in advance and keep everything else separate until you've reached your cabin or condo for the night. The original recipe calls for angelica, a common herb in Scandinavia; here we specify parsley, but if you can source angelica or, better yet, foraged herbs from the forest that surrounds your vacation dwelling, you'll taste the difference.

Bring a pot of salted water to a boil. Add the potatoes, turn the heat to medium, and simmer until the potatoes are just tender, about 12 minutes. Drain. Once the potatoes are cool enough to handle, break them apart using your fingers.

Bring a medium pot of salted water to a boil. Turn the heat to medium, carefully lower in the eggs using a slotted spoon, and simmer for 6 minutes. Remove the eggs from the water using the slotted spoon and transfer to a bowl. Run cold water over the eggs until they are cooled to room temperature and then carefully peel them. The eggs yolks will have just begun to set, so the eggs will be quite delicate; peel as gently and deftly as you can.

In a nonstick skillet over medium heat, melt the butter. Add the potatoes, shallot, capers, parsley, and mustard and season with vinegar and salt. Stir until everything is well coated with butter. Spoon onto six plates and top each with an egg before serving.

Smørrebrød with Shredded Pork, Pickled Cabbage, and Horseradish Mayonnaise

MAKES 12 TO 16 *SMØRREBRØD*

4 pounds pork belly

3 quarts chicken stock

2 cups low-sodium soy sauce

1 cup apple cider vinegar, plus more as needed

1 cup water

2 tablespoons granulated sugar

½ head green cabbage, cored and thinly sliced

Kosher salt

2 egg yolks

¾ cup canola oil

1 tablespoon freshly grated horseradish or 2 teaspoons prepared horseradish

2 tablespoons butter

Six 1-inch slices sourdough bread

Thinly sliced scallions for garnish

Smørrebrød ("smore-brode"), or open-faced sandwiches, are beloved throughout Scandinavia. They're often served on cozy evenings with friends, since they're easy to throw together and fun to eat. With a little planning, the recipe is also easy to bring on the road. The pork needs to cook low and slow in the oven, and the cabbage requires overnight pickling; plan to do both the day before the trip, then pack up everything in separate containers and stow it in your cooler. The pork and cabbage will keep for up to three days. At the end of a long travel day, there's nothing better than this sandwich to quell hunger and ensure that everyone's cozy.

Preheat the oven to 250°F.

Place the pork belly, fat-side up, in a roasting pan. Pour the chicken stock and soy sauce over the pork, cover with aluminum foil, and cook until the meat shreds easily, 8 to 10 hours.

In a pot, combine the vinegar, water, and sugar and bring to a boil. Turn the heat to low and simmer the pickling juice until the sugar is dissolved.

In a large bowl, toss the cabbage with 2 teaspoons salt, then pour the pickling juice over it. Cover with aluminum foil and set aside at room temperature for 6 hours. Drain the pickled cabbage and refrigerate in a covered container until ready to serve.

Remove the pork belly from the cooking liquids. Once the pork is cool enough to handle but still warm, shred it as finely as possible using your fingers.

In a stand mixer fitted with the whisk attachment, whisk the egg yolks while adding the canola oil in a slow, steady stream. Continue to whisk until a mayonnaise is emulsified. Stir in the horseradish and season with salt and vinegar.

continued

Smørrebrød with Shredded Pork, Pickled Cabbage, and Horseradish Mayonnaise

Preheat the oven to 350°F.

In a nonstick skillet over medium-high heat, melt the butter until it is bubbling and golden brown. Add the shredded pork and cook until heated through. Toast the sourdough in the oven until the edges are crispy, about 5 minutes.

Generously spread each bread slice with the mayonnaise, top with enough pork to cover, and spoon the pickled cabbage over it. Garnish with scallions. Serve while the pork and bread are still warm.

Here are a few more ideas for smørrebrød that are sure to please:

• Melt Jarlsberg cheese on top of a slice of sourdough bread until it is golden brown. Top with arugula, slices of prosciutto, and a fried egg.

• In a bowl, stir together ½ cup softened cream cheese, ½ teaspoon garlic powder, and 1 thinly sliced scallion. Season with salt and pepper. Spread over a slice of sweet rye bread and top with a few slices of smoked herring or mackerel.

• Spread a thick layer of softened butter over a crusty slice of toasted sourdough bread. Top with two slices of goat cheese, four or five sundried tomatoes, and thinly sliced basil leaves. Drizzle with a syrupy balsamic vinegar.

• In a bowl, stir together half a can of albacore tuna (preserved in water) with 1 tablespoon mayonnaise, 1 teaspoon stone-ground mustard, and 1 tablespoon capers. Season with salt and pepper. Melt Parmesan cheese on top of a slice of wheat bread and top with a few slices of red onion and the tuna.

• In a bowl, stir together ¼ cup softened cream cheese and 1 teaspoon horseradish. Season with salt and pepper. Spread over a slice of sweet rye bread. Top with thinly sliced cucumbers and a few slices of smoked salmon. Garnish with fresh dill.

SMØRREBRØD

It is said that Scandinavian farmers invented the iconic open-faced sandwiches called *smørrebrød*, which date back at least two hundred years. They brought their dinner leftovers with them to the fields in the morning along with slices of rye bread and butter to slather on top of it. The bread, which acted like a plate (the butter was a barrier between the cooking juices and the bread), was originally tossed away at the end of the meal, but eventually it, too, was consumed when it was discovered how tasty it was after it absorbed the flavorful juices. Today, smørrebrød is enjoyed throughout Scandinavia as both a breakfast and lunch staple. Denmark is the epicenter of the smørrebrød craze. Humble versions are enjoyed at casual eateries throughout the capital city of Copenhagen and more luxurious open-faced delicacies are indulged in at fine-dining restaurants.

Smørrebrød are an ideal way to lighten up a sandwich since one of the bread slices is left out of the assembly process. They are also beautiful because the ingredients are on full display. Danish rye bread, which is called *rugbrod*, is a dense, moist bread that tastes sweeter than its earthier counterpart. It sometimes contains nuts and seeds, which add lovely texture and flavor. It's available in many grocery stores and at artisan bread bakeries. If you have a difficult time sourcing it, substitute the bread of your choice. Because rugbrod is more fragile than most bread, there is a chance it could crumble in a traditional toaster, so a toaster oven or standard oven are therefore recommended. There is also a recipe for a more substantial open-faced sandwich and additional smørrebrød ideas on page 137.

Open-Faced Rye Bread Sandwiches with Cottage Cheese and Pickled and Salted Radishes

MAKES 4 SANDWICHES

6 radishes, rinsed and thinly sliced

1 cup warm water

1 tablespoon apple cider or distilled white vinegar

1 tablespoon granulated sugar

Kosher salt

1 cup cottage cheese

1 scallion, thinly sliced

Softened butter for serving

4 slices sweet rye bread, toasted

This recipe is a simple construction of toasted rye bread, butter, cottage cheese, and pickled and salted radishes. The pickled radishes are a cinch to prepare and are ready in minutes because they do not require the traditional pickling method of heating the liquid before it is poured on top of the vegetables. They are crisp and refreshing with an energetic zing of vinegar balanced by the sugar. For something a little more substantial, layer a slice or two of thinly sliced turkey or chicken over the butter before adding the cottage cheese.

Place half the radish slices in a small nonreactive bowl. In a second bowl, whisk together the water, vinegar, sugar, and a pinch of salt until the sugar and salt dissolve. Pour over the radishes. Let stand at room temperature for 30 minutes and then drain before serving.

In a bowl, gently stir together the cottage cheese and scallion Season with salt. Spread a thick layer of butter over the toasted bread slices and top each one with a generous spoonful of cottage cheese. Sprinkle the remaining radishes with salt and then arrange both the pickled and salted radishes artfully over the cottage cheese. Serve immediately.

Marinated Herring on Rye Bread with Eggs and Shallot

SERVES 6

6 tablespoons butter, at room temperature

6 tablespoons crème fraîche

6 slices Danish rye bread

One 16-ounce jar premium pickled herring

3 hard-boiled eggs, peeled and halved

1 shallot, thinly sliced

Watercress or parsley leaves for garnish

Herring has been a beloved mainstay of the Scandinavian diet for centuries. A jar of it is easy to take on the road for a picnic or trip, and it will keep for at least a week if it's chilled. A favorite way to serve it in Iceland and other Nordic nations is with rich, high-quality butter slathered on rye bread. (Braud & Co. in Reykjavík makes our favorite rye bread—look locally for one that's moist, deep brown, and slightly sweet. Based on your preference, it could be crusted with seeds or nuts for additional texture.) This recipe takes it a step further by adding hard-boiled eggs, crème fraîche, and thinly sliced shallot. Select herring pickled with vegetables to use as a garnish and add a smattering of citrusy greens such as watercress or parsley. Serve with a chilled pint of light beer, like a pilsner or a hard cider.

In a nonstick pan over medium heat, melt 2 tablespoons of the butter until it is bubbling and golden brown. Let cool to room temperature.

Transfer the brown butter to a bowl along with the crème fraîche and whip with a fork until incorporated. Cover with plastic wrap and refrigerate until chilled.

Smear each slice of bread with some of the remaining 4 tablespoons butter. Top with herring and half an egg, and garnish with the shallot and watercress. Spoon a dollop of the brown butter cream on top. Serve immediately.

GARDENING WITH KIDS

Most children love to get their hands dirty. Even the smallest patch of soil can teach your kids about where their food comes from, the cycle of life, and healthful eating. A carrot pulled from their own garden is much more tantalizing than a bunch picked up at the supermarket, inspiring a sense of wonder, accomplishment, and a deeper understanding about the food on their plate. Here are a few gardening projects to enjoy with your children.

- Keep an avocado pit after making a batch of guacamole; clean and dry it (they are slippery when wet!) and suspend it with three or four toothpicks over a glass of water with the pointed end up and about an inch of the round end submerged. Kids will love checking its progress as it sends out roots and a sprout.

- For a dual recycling and gardening lesson, use egg cartons as planters to grow herbs like chives or mint. Or, remove the bottom from a gallon-size water bottle, flip the bottle upside down, position a tomato seedling to grow through the spout, and fill the bottle with soil. Hang the planter spout-side down and water every couple days, or when the soil feels dry. Your kids will enjoy watching the vine's progress throughout the summer.

- For a craft project, paint stones vibrant colors. Once they are dry, create homemade garden tags by using a waterproof marker to write the name of each plant.

- For a homemade bird feeder, string O-shaped dry cereal along a long piece of twine. Hang this near the garden but close enough to a window for your kids to witness the birds feasting on their creation.

How to Raise a Butterfly

Caring for a vulnerable caterpillar until it transforms into a magnificent butterfly provides many lessons for your children. It teaches them about taking responsibility for a creature that is entirely dependant upon them for survival. It helps them understand nature's life cycle in a relatively brief period of time. It imbues wonder when the butterfly emerges from its cocoon and a sense of pride when it is set free in the garden. It also offers lessons in metamorphosis, seasonality, and migration. Most important, it is an activity that affords several awe-filled moments of connection with your child as they witness their caterpillar's transformation.

- Caterpillars tend to emerge in late spring and early summer. In the western United States, monarch caterpillars are found on milkweed, their only food source. Golden-wing tiger swallowtails are plentiful in eastern America, where they feast on a variety of trees, including paw-paws, birch, willow, ash, and cherry, along with plants such as tulips, milkweed, and lilac. Locate them with your children, using a field guide to teach about plant identification.

- Prepare a home for your caterpillar by picking up a mesh-walled butterfly house at a pet or hobby shop or design one using an old aquarium. Fashion it with a well-secured cheesecloth or mesh lid because caterpillars require abundant ventilation. Line the bottom of its home with newspaper or paper towels.

- Whether you're caring for one caterpillar or more, help your kids carefully collect each one by enticing it onto the branch or stem of its food source without handling it, they can be very sensitive to our hand oils and their delicate bodies injure easily.

- Caterpillars do not require water; they rely on the moisture from their food source to stay hydrated. For nourishment, offer several branches, leaves, and stems of their preferred vegetation and swap it out regularly to keep it fresh. Be sure that it is free of other insects before placing it in the container. If your children are old enough, put them in charge of feeding their caterpillar.

- Keep the container in a well-ventilated area out of direct sunlight. Ask your kids to mist it occasionally, but be attentive to mold growth. Swap out the newspaper or paper towels every few days to keep the area clean.

- The caterpillar will begin its transformation in a matter of days. Once it transforms into a chrysalis, be sure it is positioned in a place where it will have enough room to spread its wings as a butterfly. If not, carefully move the branch or stem to accommodate. The only thing to do now is wait. A monarch will emerge in a week or two, whereas other varieties require the entire winter. Read about the species with your children.

- Once a butterfly emerges, offer it several hours to strengthen its wings. Now it is time to set it free. If your butterfly species enjoys specific fruit or the nectar from certain flowers, help your children arrange these in your garden along with a shallow container filled with fresh water before it is time for release.

- Spend time observing your butterfly in the garden. If the species migrates, research the area where it will travel and show your kids the distance on a map. Images of the monarch migration to Central Mexico are especially dramatic and inspiring.

Quick Rhubarb Pickles

MAKES FOUR 8-OUNCE
CANNING JARS OF PICKLES

8 stalks rhubarb, trimmed to the height of the canning jar

4 cinnamon sticks

4 star anise pods

8 cloves

4 bay leaves

1 cup sugar

2 cups distilled white vinegar

1 teaspoon salt

Rhubarb is plentiful throughout Scandinavia, growing throughout the spring, and forming stalks that are thicker and sweeter than those in the United States. In northern Iceland, where Gunnar grew up, his mother used to send him out to the family rhubarb patch with a tiny bowl of sugar. As he harvested, he would dip a stalk into the sugar and munch happily. Whatever made it into the house, he would turn over to his mother, who would transform them into pickles the family would indulge in all winter long. Rest assured that U.S.-grown rhubarb works just fine in this recipe, but do taste and add more sugar if you like.

Divide the rhubarb, cinnamon, star anise, cloves, and bay leaves among four sterilized canning jars (see Note).

In a pot over high heat, combine the sugar, vinegar, and salt and bring to a boil. Turn the heat to a simmer and stir until the sugar is dissolved.

Pour the vinegar mixture over the rhubarb and let cool to room temperature. Screw the lids onto the jars and refrigerate for 48 hours before serving. The pickles will keep, refrigerated, for up to 2 weeks.

Note: To sterilize canning jars and their sealing rings, preheat the oven to 225°F, place the lids and jars (lid-side up) separately in a roasting pan, and bake for 20 minutes. Turn off the oven but leave the lids and jars inside until you are ready to fill them. Use an oven mitt to transfer the jars to a clean work surface.

THE TRANSFORMATIVE MAGIC OF PRESERVATION

Pickling the last vegetables of the season and transforming ripe summer berries into jam, stone fruit into chutney, or a basket of herbs into flavored vinegars are all ways to extend a season long after it has passed. Nearly every culture has devised ways to preserve fresh foods since the earliest days of food-gathering and cultivation. This absorbing practice invites us as cooks to stop and appreciate the generosity of nature, captures the bounty of food that would otherwise go unused, nourishes us in ways few other processes can, and connects us to the generations that came before—our grandmothers, who taught us how to make jams and pickles, and their grandmothers, who showed them how to do it, one jar at a time.

Pickling and making jam all through spring and summer transforms a season's bounty into a welcome treat for the colder months. In Scandinavia, there are rhubarb and berries in the springtime, radishes and tomatoes in the summer, root vegetables and apples in the fall. Foraging and preservation gatherings are common during the warmer months, when groups of friends venture out for rhubarb harvesting or berry picking, then spend the afternoon transforming them into pickles and jam.

PACKING FOR A PLANE OR TRAIN RIDE

Flying or embarking on a long train or plane journey doesn't have to mean suffering. Arm yourself with soothing items that will keep you organized and comfortable.

- Before you embark, give a loved one your travel agenda and contact information for when you're on the road.

- If traveling internationally, call your bank to let them know which countries you'll be in overseas to avoid cash withdrawal or purchasing headaches.

- Pack as lightly as possible and include a laundry bag and on-the-go spot remover.

- If traveling to a country with a different language, bring along a language translation book or download a translation app

- Pack appropriate electrical converters and don't forget your gadget chargers.

- Download movies or books to keep yourself entertained while in transit.

- In your underseat bag, tuck earplugs, headphones, a sleep mask, comfy socks, facial wipes, mints or gum, hand sanitizer, healthful snacks such as nuts or dried fruit, and a lightweight blanket.

- Fully charge your gadgets and check in the night before to select a comfortable seat and collect your boarding pass.

TRAVELING WITH CHILDREN

Traveling with your children instills in them a lifelong curiosity about new people, cultures, and places. Here are a few tips for creating adventures that strengthen familial bonds and conjure indelible memories.

• Talk to your children beforehand about where you are going. Read about the location and the people and sights they will encounter to kindle excitement and anticipation.

• Encourage responsibility: Give children their own small rolling suitcase to pack and carry with them throughout the journey.

• Bring along familiar comforts from home, like a blanket or stuffed animal, and pack a nightlight for bedtime reassurance.

• Encourage those who are old enough to keep a sketchbook or journal, and bring along tape and scissors so they can fill their keepsake book with things they find interesting.

• Bring games, toys, art supplies, and healthful snacks to occupy while in transit.

• Once you get to your destination, if they are young and tend to roam, use a tracking app for your own reassurance. But don't forget, wanderers make the best future travelers.

HYGGE ROAD TRIP

No matter the distance, there is nothing like a cozy road trip to reboot a harried life. Bring along a friend or two, a well-stocked cooler of food and snacks, and a well-planned playlist or audio books to sustain you through the boring stretches. Bring a power pack to keep your phone's GPS running and a good map in case you are remote enough to lose your Wi-Fi connection. Stop at tourist information booths to learn about your location, and don't skip the kooky shops and cafés you stumble upon. These are often hidden gems where you'll have the most amusing experiences. If you're in the middle of nowhere, so much the better. Have a tailgate party with local food, and take a walk afterward. There's no telling what you might discover.

OUTDOOR ENTERTAINING

Living is easy in the summertime, and entertaining reflects the spirit of joie de vivre in which all of us—particularly Scandinavians—revel during the warmer months. Midsummer in late June, the longest day of the year, is celebrated with relish throughout Scandinavia. In the countryside, bonfires blaze at summer cottages; in the cities, sidewalk parties spill into the streets. Fireworks conclude an evening of collective entertaining throughout the entire region. Grilled lamb and beef are popular foods to serve alongside chilled wine, beer, and aquavit. In Finland, the faithful still practice an ancient tradition that has single women gather seven varieties of flowers and place these under their pillows, inviting their future husbands to visit their dreams. You don't have to live in Scandinavia to embrace the principles of midsummer entertaining. Grilling and good music are musts, and a divining rod or two will add mystery and laughter to the party.

An outdoor winter party (weather permitting) can be just as merry as a summer one if you ensure that everyone is kept toasty. A daytime bonfire is a fun way to gather together around a heat source that will comfort chilly hands and toes. Fill one thermos with a warm cocktail such as a hot toddy or spiked cider, and another with hot chocolate or spiced cider. Pre-sharpen sticks and offer high-quality sausages or homemade marshmallows for toasting. Line chairs with cozy blankets, and bring a few wool hats and pairs of mittens in case anyone forgot that it's winter. Be sure you have plenty of wood to keep the fire (and party) going.

Acknowledgments

There are so many people who helped make writing this book a hyggeligt experience for us. We would like to thank our editor, Jenny Wapner, photographer, Peter Frank Edwards, creative director, Janine Ersfeld, prop stylist, Guðfinna Mjöll Magnúsdóttir, agent, Amy Collins, and designer, Ashley Lima.

Gunnar would like to thank his mother and father and especially his wife Freyja Rós Oskarsdóttir and children Hildur, Salka, and Indriði, with extra gratitude to his son Mikael who helped cook many of their favorite dishes during the writing of this book.

Jody would like to thank her beloved grandmother Evelyn Bragelman and her mother, Mary Eddy, who passed away while this book was being written. She would like to thank her family and friends who provided abundant love and comfort during this heartbreaking time, including Colleen Foster, Mark Anderson, Theresa Hillesheim, Peter Rosene, Sheila Pearson, Daniel Rosene, Matthew Rosene, Shelly Rosene, Emmelia Rosene, Anne McBride, Bridget and Ari McGinty, Maneet Chauhan, Vivek Deora, Sean Sherman, Dana Noelle Thompson, Jamie Simpson, Rita and Leon LaChapelle, Melissa Henderson, Jeanna Christiansen, Martha Holmberg, Claire Handleman, Erin and Dan Jurek, Janice and Tom Honeycutt, Pat Sweeney, Anna Painter, Susana Trilling, Ruth Alegria, Jean Stearns, Kjartan Gislason, Lois Ellen Frank, Kristin Teig, Lee and Mary Jones, Mike Ineson, Claudia Woloshin, Cortney Burns, Fernando Salazar, Paula Perlis, Raychel O'Keeffe, and Prannie Rhatigan.

We would also like to thank our many Icelandic friends who helped us realize the vision for this book in so many kind and generous ways: Villi Goði, Ólafur Örn Ólafsson, Ólafur Ágústsson, Inga Magnea Skuladottir, Björn Steinar Jónsson, Hrefna Osk Benediktsdottir, Ýmir Björgvin Arthúrsson, Muni Asgeirsson, Torfi Thór Torfason, Binni Smiður, Háfdán Pedersen, and the teams at Dill, Kex, H12, and Mikkeler & Friends.

Index

A

All Saints' Day, 127
almonds
    Fried Fish with Almonds
        and Capers, 62
    Glögg, 117
amaretto
    Birch Sour, 116
Apples, Spiced Roasted,
    Steel-Cut Oatmeal with Yogurt
    and, 32–33
arugula
    Fennel Salad with Blue Cheese
        and Walnuts, 56
    Red Beet Salad with Hazelnuts,
        Pickled Onion, and Goat
        Cheese, 82–84
    Smoked Cheese and
        Grilled Bread with Peppery
        Greens and Lemon-Yogurt
        Dressing, 58–59
Ástarpungar (Love Balls), 107

B

barbers, 42, 48
Bath Salts, Homemade, 43
beef
    Grilled Rib-Eyes with Herb
        Butter and Capers, 95–97
Beet Salad, Red, with Hazelnuts,
    Pickled Onion, and Goat
    Cheese, 82–84
Beignets, Icelandic (Kleinur), 17
berries
    Berry Spritzers, 118
    Pancakes with Berries and
        Whipped Cream, 24–25
    Rice Porridge, 34
Birch Sour, 116
Bitters, House, 119
blueberries
    Pancakes with Berries and
        Whipped Cream, 24–25
    Rice Porridge, 34
Bok Choy, Braised Lamb Shanks
    with Sweet-and-Sour Dill Oil
    and, 93–94

Boxing Day, 129
Bratwurst with Sauerkraut and
    Smashed Potatoes, 66
bread
    Marinated Herring on Rye Bread
        with Eggs and Shallot, 142
    Smoked Cheese and
        Grilled Bread with Peppery
        Greens and Lemon-Yogurt
        Dressing, 58–59
    See also sandwiches
breakfast
    in bed, 28
    as sit-down affair, 32
brunch, 36–37
butterflies, 146–47

C

cabbage
    Lamb Stew, 91
    Smørrebrød with
        Shredded Pork, Pickled
        Cabbage, and Horseradish
        Mayonnaise, 137–38
Celeriac Puree, Baked Cod with
    Chorizo, Caramelized Onions,
    and, 85–87
cheese
    Blackened Salmon with
        Cottage Cheese and Cider
        Vinaigrette, 88
    Fennel Salad with Blue Cheese
        and Walnuts, 56
    Open-Faced Rye Bread
        Sandwiches with Cottage
        Cheese and Pickled and
        Salted Radishes, 141
    Red Beet Salad with Hazelnuts,
        Pickled Onion, and Goat
        Cheese, 82–84
    Smoked Cheese and
        Grilled Bread with Peppery
        Greens and Lemon-Yogurt
        Dressing, 58–59
children
    butterflies and, 146–47
    gardening with, 132, 145
    traveling with, 131, 152

chocolate
    Hot Chocolate, 71
    Kökur (Icelandic Cookies), 105
    Meringue Buttons, 104
    Orange and Chocolate
        Cookies, 108
Christmas Eve and Christmas
    Day, 128–29
cocktail parties, 113. *See also* drinks
coconut
    Meringue Buttons, 104
cod
    Baked Cod with Celeriac Puree,
        Chorizo, and Caramelized
        Onions, 85–87
    Fried Fish with Almonds and
        Capers, 62
coffee, 10, 12–14
cookies
    Ginger Cookies, 109
    Kökur (Icelandic Cookies), 105
    Orange and Chocolate
        Cookies, 108
    parties, 102

D

date night, 73
drinks
    Berry Spritzers, 118
    Birch Sour, 116
    Glögg, 117
    Hot Chocolate, 71
    Rhubarb and Lemon Balm
        Smoothie, 35
    The Tom Cat, 114

E

Easter, 126
eggs
    Marinated Herring on Rye Bread
        with Eggs and Shallot, 142
    Poached Eggs and Watercress
        with Pickled Shallots and
        Horseradish, 53–54
    Smoked Cheese and
        Grilled Bread with Peppery
        Greens and Lemon-Yogurt
        Dressing, 58–59

entertaining
    cocktail parties, 113
    cookie parties, 102
    game nights, 100–101
    in hyggeligt way, 75–76
    outdoor, 132, 154
    parting gifts, 79, 81, 119
    pizza parties, 99

F
Fastelavn, 125
Fennel Salad with Blue Cheese
    and Walnuts, 56
fish
    Baked Cod with Celeriac Puree,
      Chorizo, and Caramelized
      Onions, 85–87
    Blackened Salmon with
      Cottage Cheese and Cider
      Vinaigrette, 88
    Fried Fish with Almonds and
      Capers, 62
    Marinated Herring on Rye Bread
      with Eggs and Shallot, 142
    Potato Soup with Smoked
      Haddock and Dill, 60–61
    Salmon with Baby Potatoes
      and Pine, 64
Fritters, Spiced Buttermilk, 20–21

G
game nights, 100–101
gardening with children, 132, 145
gifts, 79, 81, 119
gin
    The Tom Cat, 114
Ginger Cookies, 109
Glögg, 117
grapefruit
    House Bitters, 119
grooming, 42, 48

H
Haddock, Smoked, Potato Soup
    with Dill and, 60–61

hazelnuts, 58
    Red Beet Salad with Hazelnuts,
      Pickled Onion, and Goat
      Cheese, 82–84
    Rice Porridge, 34
Herring, Marinated, on Rye Bread
    with Eggs and Shallot, 142
hiking, 19
holidays, 75–76, 124–29
horseradish, 53
House Bitters, 119
hygge, concept of, 1–3, 7

K
Kleinur (Icelandic Beignets), 17
Kökur (Icelandic Cookies), 105

L
lamb
    Braised Lamb Shanks with Bok
      Choy and Sweet-and-Sour Dill
      Oil, 93–94
    Lamb Stew, 91
Laufabrauð, 110–11
lemon balm, 35
Lemon-Yogurt Dressing, 59
Love Balls (Ástarpungar), 107

M
Meringue Buttons, 104
mesclun
    Fennel Salad with Blue Cheese
      and Walnuts, 56
    Red Beet Salad with Hazelnuts,
      Pickled Onion, and Goat
      Cheese, 82–84
mezcal
    The Tom Cat, 114
Midsummer, 126
movie night, 68
Mushrooms, Oyster, Braised
    Pork Tenderloin with Parsnips
    and, 65

N
New Year's Eve, 129

O
Oatmeal, Steel-Cut, with
    Yogurt and Spiced Roasted
    Apples, 32–33
oranges
    House Bitters, 119
    Orange and Chocolate
      Cookies, 108
ornaments, 123
outdoor entertaining, 132, 154

P
packing, 151
Pancakes with Berries and
    Whipped Cream, 24–25
parsnips
    Baked Cod with Celeriac Puree,
      Chorizo, and Caramelized
      Onions, 85–87
    Braised Pork Tenderloin with
      Oyster Mushrooms and
      Parsnips, 65
parting gifts, 79, 81, 119
pickles, 149
    Quick Rhubarb Pickles, 148
picnics, 135
pizza parties, 99
Popcorn, Stove-Top, 69
pork
    Braised Pork Tenderloin with
      Oyster Mushrooms and
      Parsnips, 65
    Smørrebrød with
      Shredded Pork, Pickled
      Cabbage, and Horseradish
      Mayonnaise, 137–38
    See also sausage
Porridge, Rice, 34
potatoes
    Bratwurst with Sauerkraut
      and Smashed Potatoes, 66
    Lamb Stew, 91
    Potato Soup with Smoked
      Haddock and Dill, 60–61
    Salmon with Baby Potatoes
      and Pine, 64
    Warm Potato Salad, 136

R

Radishes, Pickled and Salted, Open-Faced Rye Bread Sandwiches with Cottage Cheese and, 141

raspberries
Rice Porridge, 34

rhubarb
Quick Rhubarb Pickles, 148
Rhubarb and Lemon Balm Smoothie, 35

Rice Porridge, 34

road trips, 132, 153

rum
House Bitters, 119

S

St. Knut's Day, 124
St. Lucia's Day, 127
St. Martin's Day, 127
St. Stephen's Day, 129

salads
Fennel Salad with Blue Cheese and Walnuts, 56
Red Beet Salad with Hazelnuts, Pickled Onion, and Goat Cheese, 82–84
Warm Potato Salad, 136

salmon
Blackened Salmon with Cottage Cheese and Cider Vinaigrette, 88
Salmon with Baby Potatoes and Pine, 64

Salts, Homemade Bath, 43

sandwiches
Open-Faced Rye Bread Sandwiches with Cottage Cheese and Pickled and Salted Radishes, 141
Smørrebrød with Shredded Pork, Pickled Cabbage, and Horseradish Mayonnaise, 137–38, 140

Sauerkraut, Bratwurst with Smashed Potatoes and, 66

saunas, 45

sausage
Baked Cod with Celeriac Puree, Chorizo, and Caramelized Onions, 85–87
Bratwurst with Sauerkraut and Smashed Potatoes, 66

schnapps
Birch Sour, 116

self-care, 41–42

Shallots, Pickled, 53

sherry
The Tom Cat, 114

Shrovetide, 125

Smoothie, Rhubarb and Lemon Balm, 35

smørrebrød, 140
Smørrebrød with Shredded Pork, Pickled Cabbage, and Horseradish Mayonnaise, 137–38

Soup, Potato, with Smoked Haddock and Dill, 60–61

spaces, cozy, 42, 46

spa treatments, 41

spinach
Fennel Salad with Blue Cheese and Walnuts, 56
Red Beet Salad with Hazelnuts, Pickled Onion, and Goat Cheese, 82–84

staying in, 51–52

sugar, aromatic, 81

T

tea, 10, 14–15
Thorrablot, 124–25
The Tom Cat, 114
travel
with children, 131, 152
packing for, 151
road trips, 132, 153

V

vermouth
The Tom Cat, 114

vodka
Glögg, 117

W

walnuts, 58
Fennel Salad with Blue Cheese and Walnuts, 56
Rice Porridge, 34
Smoked Cheese and Grilled Bread with Peppery Greens and Lemon-Yogurt Dressing, 58–59

Walpurgis Night, 126

Watercress, Poached Eggs and, with Pickled Shallots and Horseradish, 53–54

weeknight meals and activities, 51–52

whisky
Birch Sour, 116

wine
Glögg, 117

Y

yogurt
Lemon-Yogurt Dressing, 59
Rhubarb and Lemon Balm Smoothie, 35
Steel-Cut Oatmeal with Yogurt and Spiced Roasted Apples, 32–33

Published in the United States by Ten Speed Press,
an imprint of the Crown Publishing Group,
a division of Penguin Random House LLC, New York.
www.crownpublishing.com
www.tenspeed.com

Ten Speed Press and the Ten Speed Press colophon are registered trademarks of Penguin Random House LLC.

Library of Congress Cataloging-in-Publication Data is on file with the publisher.

Hardcover ISBN: 978-0-399-57993-6
eBook ISBN: 978-0-399-57994-3

Printed in China

Design by Ashley Lima

10 9 8 7 6 5 4 3 2 1

First Edition

3 1333 04648 0271